MW01044471

BALTIMORE
IN THE
CIVIL WAR

BALTIMORE
IN THE
CIVIL WAR

THE PRATT STREET RIOT AND
A CITY OCCUPIED

HARRY A. EZRATTY

Charleston London

THE
History
PRESS

Published by The History Press
Charleston, SC 29403
www.historypress.net

Copyright © 2010 by Harry A. Ezratty
All rights reserved

Cover images: Courtesy of Enoch Pratt Free Library, Maryland's State Resource Center,
Baltimore, MD.

First published 2010
Second printing 2012
Third printing 2012

Manufactured in the United States

ISBN 978.1.60949.003.4

Library of Congress Cataloging-in-Publication Data

Ezratty, Harry A.
Baltimore in the Civil War : the Pratt Street riot and a city occupied / Harry A. Ezratty.
p. cm.
Includes bibliographical references.
ISBN 978-1-60949-003-4
1. Baltimore (Md.)--History--Civil War, 1861-1865. 2. Riots--Maryland--Baltimore--
History--19th century. 3. Baltimore (Md.)--History--Civil War, 1861-1865--Social aspects.
4. United States--History--Civil War, 1861-1865--Social aspects. I. Title.
F189.B157E98 2010
975.2'603--dc22
2010030904

Notice: The information in this book is true and complete to the best of our knowledge. It is
offered without guarantee on the part of the author or The History Press. The author and
The History Press disclaim all liability in connection with the use of this book.

All rights reserved. No part of this book may be reproduced or transmitted in any form
whatsoever without prior written permission from the publisher except in the case of brief
quotations embodied in critical articles and reviews.

To the men and the women who died in the Civil War
The Blue and the Gray: Americans all
and
To the City of Baltimore

Contents

Contents

Foreword

I'll be the first to admit that I am an unlikely person to write a foreword to a book about Baltimore's Pratt Street Riot. My background is in neither U.S. Civil War nor legal history but rather the history of architecture and the built environment. While many people focus on personalities, events or political or intellectual patterns or currents, and lean on them to illuminate the past, I tend to focus on the man-made backdrop against which human events took place. It goes without saying that architecture and, more generally, the built environment—buildings, parks, roads, bridges and other structures and places—define communities and give them their identities. Brantz Mayer, a prominent Baltimore-born and based historian and writer, said as much in 1848 when he remarked, on the occasion of the opening of the Baltimore Athenaeum, a leading cultural institution of its day, "Architecture is the physiognomy of cities." But the built environment is more than a mere representation of communities. It is also an agent in shaping and directing human behaviors and events.

The question posed by Harry Ezratty in his preface of why some native Baltimoreans are unaware of the Pratt Street Riot and other major events in the history of Baltimore is a complicated one with many plausible answers. Students might not be learning about it in schools. Local history organizations and institutions might not be highlighting it in publications and exhibits. The tourism and promotion bureau might not be promoting it. Add to these the tendency for people to take their immediate surroundings for granted and to visit museums, parks and other cultural attractions while on vacation in other places than at home. (Transplants like Ezratty and others, myself included, who grew up somewhere else but at some point in their lives established roots in Baltimore, tend to research and explore their adopted communities more actively than the natives. It's part of the acculturation process, which for many transplants may last a lifetime.) Native Baltimoreans—anyone for that matter—also might be unaware of the riot because so little of the built environment that formed the backdrop of that pivotal event in the history of the Civil War survives. The medieval idiom, "Out of sight, out of mind," comes to mind. Certainly, people and events are important, but the places where history took place help cement those stories in people's memories.

The absence of that architectural backdrop certainly helps explain the difficulty of addressing the riot and, by extension, the Civil War when teaching place-based history or the history of architecture in Baltimore. Unlike in Washington, D.C., where the construction of the dome of the U.S. Capitol continued uninterrupted throughout the Civil War, in Baltimore the construction and completion of major monuments came to a grinding halt in 1861. The Baltimore City Hall—arguably the city's most important construction project of the mid-nineteenth century—got as far as the design stage in 1860, but construction did not begin on the site until 1867, by which time both the building committee membership and architectural tastes had changed. As built, the city hall, which features mansard roofs that were in fashion in Baltimore after the Civil War, bears little resemblance to the approved antebellum design. That in and of itself is significant and worthwhile, but it represents a caesura or a breach in the history of Baltimore's architecture, not a continuity or bridge across the 1860s.

The Peabody Institute, a cultural institution founded by the international financier and philanthropist George Peabody, though completed in 1861 on Baltimore's Mount Vernon Place, stood dormant for the duration of the war; it finally opened its doors in 1866, five years after the building was complete. One noteworthy exception to this building bust in Baltimore was the Classical revival U.S. Courthouse built on the northwest corner of Fayette Street and Guilford Avenue between 1862 and 1865, but it did not survive beyond the 1930s.

The Civil War camps established throughout Baltimore by Union regiments in the early 1860s have long since faded into oblivion. Nothing remains of Camp Carroll at Mount Clare, the mid-eighteenth-century country estate of Charles Carroll, barrister, a distant cousin of Charles Carroll of Carrollton, a Marylander and the only Catholic signer of the Declaration of Independence. Camps Bradford and Millington, the

Lafayette and Belger Barracks, the camp of the Twenty-first Indiana Regiment at Druid Hill and all the military hospitals in occupied Baltimore, some of them in purpose-built buildings and others in preexisting ones, are all gone, though the sites—some of them city parks—remain.

Of course, a number of key buildings and sites in Baltimore associated with the people and events of the Civil War survive. Federal Hill, the site directly across the Basin (now the Inner Harbor) from Baltimore's main wharves, where Union general Benjamin F. Butler and a Massachusetts regiment built earthworks and established a fort, is now a popular city park. Fort McHenry, now a national park and historic shrine, served as a prison where many Southern sympathizers ended up being held without charge after President Abraham Lincoln's suspension of the writ of habeas corpus on April 27, 1861. However, the fort is first and foremost recognized as the "birthplace of the national anthem" and for its role in repelling the British and defending the city of Baltimore during the War of 1812.

Both President Street and Camden railroad stations—the bookends of that fatal trajectory along which the Pratt Street Riot took place and people died—still stand, though stripped of their train sheds and now serving other purposes. President Street Station is now home to the Baltimore Civil War Museum, which has struggled to survive ever since it first opened its doors in 1997. Camden Station, today an architectural pendant to Baltimore's Oriole Park at Camden Yards baseball stadium, houses a sports museum.

The ruins of Glen Ellen, the nation's first Gothic revival country estate, likewise survive. Harry Gilmor, the Baltimore County cavalryman, Southern sympathizer and, ultimately, Confederate soldier who laid waste to some of Baltimore's transportation infrastructure in the aftermath of the riot and in successive campaigns during the Civil War, had inherited the house from his father in the 1870s. Covered in thick vegetation and inaccessible to all but the most intrepid hikers and mountain bikers (the site is within the city-owned and restricted Loch Raven Reservoir in Baltimore County), the ruins of the house where Harry lived and then died in the 1880s are, for the most part, off the radar.

Many other mansions, town houses, country estates and properties owned by people tied to the events of the Civil War still stand in Baltimore City and the surrounding metropolitan area, but by continuing in that direction I would be dancing around the problem at hand—that of the Pratt Street Riot and the difficulty of establishing an architectural context of the event of sufficient visual force that people can envision it and comprehend why it took place when and where it did.

Pratt Street—the street along which that mob of Southern sympathizers and the Sixth Massachusetts Volunteers came to blows on April 19, 1861, leaving four soldiers and twelve civilians dead and more than thirty-six people wounded—had been part of the Baltimore street grid since the late eighteenth century, though the stretch of street in question came about piecemeal roughly between 1780 and 1812 (the section of Pratt between Hanover Street and the Jones Falls sits on land reclaimed from the harbor). Although Baltimore Street (also called Market Street), which runs east–west and parallel to Pratt Street, was the city's main commercial street, Pratt connected the rest of the city to the wharves. Pratt Street still marks that important border in downtown Baltimore between land and sea, though the warehouses and sailing ships are long gone, replaced by the Inner Harbor, the pioneering, late twentieth-century waterfront festival marketplace of food and shopping pavilions, luxury hotels and office buildings, restaurants, museums and other tourist attractions.

Many other important aspects of Pratt Street have changed since 1861. The street is much wider, paved, completely given over to cars, trucks and buses that sometimes race but mostly crawl in one direction, passing through countless traffic lights, from west to east. Today's traffic pattern on Pratt Street hardly makes interpreting the Pratt Street Riot easy, since traffic now moves in the opposite direction of those horse-drawn rail cars that attempted to carry the Massachusetts volunteers from President Street Station in the east end of downtown Baltimore to Camden Station in the west end.

As for those horse-drawn rail cars, they are things of the past. Although you might see the occasional horse-drawn carriage carrying tourists from one end of the Inner Harbor to the other, those rails upon which the nineteenth-century rail cars carrying those Massachusetts soldiers depended and which the angry mob sabotaged, are long gone.

Even the buildings that formed the architectural backdrop of the riot and in which many rioters and observers sought shelter when things got bloody are gone. The Great Fire of February 7–8, 1904—another pivotal event in the history of Baltimore that, as Ezratty notes, few native Baltimoreans know much about—consumed twenty-four blocks in the city's central business district, including Pratt Street and the wharves. According to the news reports, the fire had damaged or destroyed more than fifteen hundred buildings, affected twenty-five hundred businesses and cost about thirty-five thousand people their jobs. The memory of the fire is preserved in the street grid, just as the memory of the Pratt Street Riot is there on its street, but the gravity of both events is much more easily grasped in three dimensions than in two.

Which is why, for the purposes of this book at least, E. Sachse & Company's 1869 *Bird's-eye View of the City of Baltimore* is such a critical document for placing the Pratt Street Riot in its urban context. Although a two-dimensional print, the Sachse bird's-eye view, begun around 1865, lays out the post–Civil War city in masterful top-down perspective. A German immigrant and pioneering lithographer living in Baltimore during the Civil War (whose shop was on the southwest corner of Camden and Charles Streets, a mere two blocks from the intersection of Pratt and Light Streets where the four soldiers of the Sixth Massachusetts were shot, beaten or stoned and subsequently died), Edward Sachse created a number of bird's-eye views, including ones of Annapolis and Ellicott Mills (now Ellicott City), but his view of Baltimore was his most ambitious. Measuring five and a half by twelve feet, the twelve-panel view of the city from the south took more than three years and four sets of hands to complete. It covers every quarter, identifies major landmarks and businesses (especially those that paid for advertising space on the map) and represents individual buildings, roads, wharves and other elements of the built environment in exacting detail, including railroad stations and rail lines.

The Sachse depicts the full extent and scale of both the President Street and Camden railroad stations, including their massive train sheds. It even shows the horse-drawn rail cars and line extending up President Street and west along Pratt that countless travelers, including the Sixth Massachusetts, used in transit between the Baltimore terminus of the Philadelphia, Wilmington and Baltimore Railroad, which connected Baltimore to the North, to the Baltimore terminus of the Baltimore & Ohio (B&O) Railroad, which connected Baltimore to the West and the South.

Looking at the Sachse with an eye toward understanding the ebb and flow of the mob and the rail cars as the Sixth Massachusetts attempted to cross a major swath of Baltimore, one gets a better sense not only of the distance those soldiers had to travel but also of the number of opportunities that the mob had to impede their movement and thus prevent their arrival to their final destination—Camden Station and, ultimately, the nation's capital. Sachse also captured the three- and four-story brick wholesale stores, town houses and warehouses that lined Pratt Street on the north, the cavernous wharves extending southward from Pratt into the harbor and the tangle of masts and lines of the ships docked in between that provided the backdrop for the deadly riot and omen of things to come. Of course, even the most exquisitely crafted bird's-eye view of mid-nineteenth-century Pratt Street is a poor substitute for the real thing. But considering the alternative of walking down a modern Pratt Street without any visual cues, a close read of this book, careful study of the Sachse stretch of road between the two stations and a look at the Currier and Ives and other prints and engravings of the period showing the human dimension of the tragedy can go a long way toward creating a vivid and lasting impression of the event and its importance in the history of Baltimore and the nation.

Before the era of railroad consolidation, Baltimore and many other major American cities issued charters to multiple private railroad companies, granting them permission to operate within city limits, which in turn connected the cities to other markets in the United States and beyond. In Baltimore, the engineers charged in 1828 with the task of laying down the route of the nation's first railroad, the B&O, made sure that the main line steered clear of heavily trafficked commercial corridors such as Baltimore and Pratt Streets. When pressures surfaced in the 1830s to establish a major freight line running along Pratt from the west end to the termini of new company lines emerging in the east, including that of the Baltimore & Port Deposit Railroad, the precursor to the Philadelphia, Wilmington & Baltimore Railroad that terminated at President Street Station, city council members, supported by many unemployed mechanics and laborers, pushed back, insisting that by preserving the cross-town transit network of horse-drawn carts and rail cars they were saving the middlemen's jobs. In the interests of commercial harmony and job preservation, Baltimore ended up with a disjointed rail transportation system.

Of course, Baltimore wasn't the only major American city transfigured and subsequently ensnarled by a convergence of independent rail lines. Like New York (including Brooklyn) and Philadelphia—the two other continental metropolises of the time—Baltimore was a "center." Situated where the land met the sea and located farther west and south than the major cities of the Northeast, the much-hailed "metropolis of the South and entrepôt of the imperial West" aspired to greatness as a destination and a gateway, certainly not an intermediate stop between the cities of the Northeast and a national capital less than half its size.

Soon after the Civil War, John Weishampel remarked in his 1866 *New Monumental City Guide* to Baltimore:

> *The commercial position of Baltimore places her in the front rank of American cities. Her location is central upon the Atlantic coast of the United States…While the Baltimore and Philadelphia Railroad affords an avenue to the East; the Central to the North; the Washington to the*

South; the various lines of steamers to all parts of the coast; the Bay to the great highway of mankind, the ocean; the Baltimore and Ohio Railroad furnishes her the key to the great West.

In brief, Baltimore at the time of the Pratt Street Riots was a transportation hub from which other roads, sea routes and rail lines radiated. That anyone or anything might bypass Baltimore while in transit between the Northeast and the South and the West was beyond the comprehension of the hundreds of thousands of people living in the city in the mid-nineteenth century, not to mention the millions of people who made up the states of the Union and those in rebellion in the South in 1861. It was as if the complicated network of independent railroads and connective horse-drawn rail lines, which characterized transportation in Baltimore in the 1860s and set the stage for the first fatal confrontation of the U.S. Civil War, was not so much an accident of history as a product of design.

Martin Perschler
Lecturer, Baltimore Architectural History
Johns Hopkins University

Preface

I'm a New Yorker who has fallen in love with Baltimore. I enjoy walking along her streets, marveling at the old brownstones that have survived the wrecker's ball. They still display the delicate and irreplaceable hand-cut stonework running across their façades. The grand nineteenth-century mansions fascinate me with their intricately carved wooden doors and the windows, some with their original hand-blown glass, fashioned in the nineteenth century. The windows soar high above the street, and as I look through them, I see glittering, multicolored, crystal-prismed chandeliers, ornate marble fireplaces and the intricate moldings that frame bookcases and paintings hung along high-ceilinged walls. I do not intrude. The proud owners of these homes pull back their drapes to invite passing strollers to look into their homes so that they may be carried back across the centuries to when much of upper-class Baltimore looked like this.

I glance at streets lined with Baltimore's famous scrubbed-white marble steps leading into row houses. Gleaming in a bright day's sun, the steps form the precise and sharp geometric patterns of stacked tiles. Many of these buildings have witnessed much of the city's dramatic history.

Baltimore is truly a living museum.

Despite such daily contact with their historic past, some native Baltimoreans admit they are unaware of some of the important events in their city's history. Friends tell me they know little or nothing of the Great Fire of 1904 that reduced much of the city's downtown section to ash, rubble and the standing skeletons of ruined buildings. The fire established traffic and street patterns with which Baltimoreans live to this day. More tell me that they have never heard of the Pratt Street Riot of 1861.

The Pratt Street Riot was a seminal event in American history, not only for Baltimore, but for America and its constitutional development as well. On April 19, 1861, when the riot broke loose in Baltimore, Abraham Lincoln had been president little more than a month. On April 12, America's new leader was suddenly faced with outright insurrection and rebellion when secessionist South Carolina ordered Union troops to surrender Fort Sumter to the breakaway state. Lincoln's refusal to give in caused the first shots of the Civil War to be fired. No blood was drawn on that day. The war's first blood would run along the cobbled streets of Baltimore a week later, on April 19, 1861, in an angry and deadly pro-Southern riot. The mob that had assembled that day underscored the feelings of many irate Baltimoreans, who refused to allow troops to pass through their city as they believed the soldiers were on their way to fight Southern sister states. Because of the Pratt Street Riot, Lincoln was faced with several serious problems.

The distance between Washington and Baltimore is less than forty miles. In 1861, the only means of traveling by railroad between Washington and the Northern states was to use the Baltimore and Ohio line, located at Camden Station in southwest Baltimore. The riot's purpose was to deny that use to Union soldiers. It almost succeeded, because for a time all movement between the North and Washington had been cut off by the destruction of road, rail and telegraph. That situation could not be allowed to continue. In order to defend the city of Washington, the Baltimore and Ohio had to continue operating without any interference. This strategic corridor had to remain open to allow soldiers to freely move on to Washington.

Lincoln also had to keep Maryland out of the Southern camp of growing secessionist states. Otherwise, Washington could become an American capital behind enemy lines. Lincoln's other unthinkable option was that he might have to abandon Washington altogether. There was no doubt that Baltimore had to be calmed down to prevent the loss of the capital city. Americans were waiting to see how their new president, a political neophyte, would handle this growing problem—one of the first and one of the most pressing of his entire four-year administration as it involved a military and constitutional crisis.

To resolve these predicaments, Lincoln would become the first American president to suspend the right to habeas corpus (Latin for "you have the body"), a legal concept requiring that a person be formally charged with a crime. If no charge is made then he must be released. Lincoln also imposed martial law on Baltimore and parts of Maryland. Later in the Civil War, he placed every Northern state under military control, suspending habeas corpus as well. These were the legacies of the Pratt Street Riot that were to last for the remainder of the Civil War and leave a scar on the city for a time after that. Following the Pratt Street Riot, America watched as Lincoln's army arrested newspapermen, state legislators, congressmen, judges, a mayor, a police chief and his board of commissioners and dozens upon dozens of private citizens, many prominent in their communities. It was all illegal, executed without proper warrants or formal charges. Some arrests were so capricious that after several months some of the unfortunates were released with no explanation as to why they had been arrested.

Lincoln would defy the Supreme Court of the United States, which tried unsuccessfully to stop him from suspending habeas corpus. He continued on this road because he felt he had little choice. He believed that had he released the prisoners, as the court ordered him to do, he would have most certainly put his country at peril.

The Pratt Street Riot also placed Baltimore under unwanted military control. Wherever Baltimoreans went in their city, they were reminded that they were living under arms. Cannons on Federal Hill, overlooking the city and its vital harbor and business district, aimed down upon them, ready to fire if needed. Patterson Park and other strategic locations throughout the city were converted from peaceful parks and other places into military installations. Baltimore was being closely and carefully watched. The city was, in Lincoln's own dramatic words, uttered during the Lincoln-Douglas debates three years earlier: "A house divided."

Today, strolling through Baltimore you can still see the places where history was made during the Civil War. Federal Hill still looms across the city's harbor. A reminder of its military role during the Civil War remains

Federal Hill before the Pratt Street Riot. *Courtesy Pratt Street Free Library, Maryland's State Resource Center, Baltimore, MD.*

Camp Carroll. This camp was erected on Patterson Park in Baltimore's Highland Town section. *Courtesy Enoch Pratt Free Library, Maryland's State Resource Center, Baltimore, MD.*

Camp Washburn, one of the several military posts located on public land after the riot. *Courtesy Enoch Pratt Free Library, Maryland's State Resource Center, Baltimore, MD.*

with the presence of now obsolete museum-type cannons set along the crest of the hill. Fort McHenry continues to guard the entrance to Baltimore Harbor, as it has for over two centuries. The President Street Station, where the riot began, is still there but much reduced in size. It is now a museum dedicated to telling the public the stories of the Pratt Street Riot and the

Civil War. Pratt Street still runs parallel to Baltimore's harbor but is no longer paved with cobblestones or lined with busy commercial warehouses and docks, nor does it sport the railway tracks that played such an important role in the riot. Today, Pratt Street is a venue for entertainment, reborn as part of the city's celebrated Harbor Place, and it remains as one of Baltimore's important thoroughfares. Baltimore's harbor is no longer known as "the Basin." Today, it is called the Inner Harbor. Farther to the west, where once the railway facility known as Camden Station carried passengers throughout the region, stands the home field of the Baltimore Orioles. They play baseball in a ball park appropriately named Camden Yards. The old station itself is today a museum.

A mile to the north, in the city's Mount Vernon district, the first monument in America to honor George Washington rises atop a Doric marble pedestal that has looked over the city of Baltimore since 1829. The monument is surrounded by the handsome mansions of the Civil War era. And the distinctive, rust-red Shot Tower, looking like a castle on a chess board, still stands north of the President Street Station as it did on the morning of April 19, 1861, witness to the first intentional drops of Civil

Fort McHenry before 1861. Compare this with later illustrations of the fort during the Civil War. *Courtesy of Enoch Pratt Free Library, Maryland's State Resource Center, Baltimore, MD.*

Baltimore's harbor, known as "the Basin," before 1861. *Courtesy of Enoch Pratt Free Library, Maryland's State Resource Center, Baltimore, MD.*

Monument Square as it appeared before 1861. It was then, as in 1861, the main meeting place for the city. *Courtesy of Enoch Pratt Free Library, Maryland's State Resource Center, Baltimore, MD.*

The Shot Tower.
Located near the
President Street
Station, in 1861 it
was a city landmark
and America's tallest
structure. *Courtesy of
Enoch Pratt Free Library,
Maryland's State Resource
Center, Baltimore, MD.*

War blood spilled on Pratt Street. This book is a way of getting Americans to remember their past and to understand the significant role Baltimore played during the Civil War.

Conscious of the importance of the Pratt Street Riot in American history, Baltimore Riot trail markers have been placed at the sites where important events occurred between the President Street Depot and Camden Station on that bloody day. Walking along this historic trail, one stands where history was made; one can read descriptions of the action and see images of the events just as they happened at the time.

So let us return to the city of Baltimore in April 1861. Let us see what the city was like just before America was plunged into a tragic Civil War. Let us learn how the Pratt Street Riot affected not only this great city but also the rest of America for so many years to come.

Acknowledgements

F ew writers can create a work as extensive as a book without the help of others. I am no exception. I have never written any work for publication that my wife, Barbara Tasch, a professional journalist, editor and publisher, has not reviewed and helped me polish. She gently suggests changes while urging me on. For her help I am always grateful.

I am grateful to Hannah Cassilly, my literary editor at The History Press, who with insight has not only encouraged me in this work but has also suggested some good additions and other changes that helped make this book more interesting. I thank her for her gracious patience and for our many helpful conversations that always set me on the right path at times when I thought I had strayed off the road.

The book *Baltimore & the Nineteenth of April, 1861*, by the city's mayor, George Brown, written in 1887, was an essential resource to get a political, social and eyewitness insight into the events of that dramatic day. Although there are differences between the book and other eyewitness accounts, it remains to this day the primary account of the Pratt Street Riot. I thank the *Baltimore Sun* and *New York Times* for their reportage of the day via the microfiche and the computer disk.

Many thanks to my friend, Marcus Dagan; he is not only a fine professional musician but also an accomplished photographer. Marcus took all the modern photos of the landmarks appearing in this book.

To the Enoch Pratt Free Library: my deepest thanks. This vital Baltimore community facility provided many of the fine images in this book through its Cator Collection, ably overseen by Jeff Korman, of the Maryland

Department, who helped me assemble the images I required. Thanks also to Peter Devereux, of the Maryland Department, who tracked down the drawing of the President Street Station, an image that was elsewhere in the library's collection; and to Lauren Silberman, who led me to the existence of that important drawing that shows the massive depot and its rail system used by travelers to transfer on to Camden Station.

Thanks to Marc Thomas at the library of the Maryland Historic Society, another vital and important community resource, for guiding me to the books written by participants of the riot, such as McHenry Howard, Harry Gilmor and others, that would have been difficult to locate, written as they were in the nineteenth and early twentieth centuries.

Thanks to the Library of Congress, with its vast and seemingly limitless collection of Americana that never fails to amaze me in its scope. Their prints, which are used in this book, were invaluable. Thanks to the Jewish Museum of Maryland and Mrs. Esther Weiner for helping to obtain the image of Rabbi Einhorn leaving Baltimore under threat.

Thanks go to Martin Perschler, who wrote the foreword to this book. A lecturer at Johns Hopkins University, Martin specializes in the history of Baltimore architecture. He leads the reader into much of what Baltimore looked like on April 19, 1861, and sets the scene for the feel of the city on that day and the major differences that have evolved over a century and a half.

Finally, to my publisher, The History Press, who thought enough of the subject of the Pratt Street Riot and my proposal for a book about it to allow me to go forward with this work; and to family and friends who encouraged me in this project. If I have left anyone out, it was done unwittingly. I apologize in advance.

April 19, 1861, Baltimore, Maryland

All hail to the Stars and Stripes.
—*Private Luther C. Ladd, Sixth Massachusetts, as he fell dead from a bullet*

They were running at double time, those blue-coated Yankee soldiers of the Sixth Massachusetts, answering President Abraham Lincoln's call for volunteers to defend their country against Southern secessionists. Some of these volunteers came from the same New England towns that summoned their minutemen ancestors to defend Lexington and Concord against the British. They came to Baltimore on April 19, the same month and day of the battle their grandfathers fought against the British eighty-six years earlier in 1775.

As their muskets dragged along the ground, they tried loading them so they could return fire from the angry mob. It was an almost impossible task. Powder and shot had to be jammed into musket barrels, followed by pushing a long ram rod into the barrel to tamp them down. Next, rifles had to be cocked, and then the soldiers had to locate, within a wild and active mob, the person who had fired on them. Once located, they had to aim and then shoot, all the while running for their lives. From time to time, they did stop to reload, aim and fire as military units are trained to do in combat.

Surrounding the New Englanders was a raging mob. The rioters were angry because these men had come to their town—Baltimore—on their way to invade eight Southern states that had seceded from the Union. As far as this city was concerned, they were sister states of the South, and no assistance could be offered to those who would attack them. At the corner

Soldiers of the Sixth Massachusetts and Baltimore civilians attacking each other. *Courtesy of Enoch Pratt Free Library, Maryland's State Resource Center, Baltimore, MD.*

of Pratt and Light Streets, near the city's docks, the mob finally caught up with the soldiers.

Shots were fired from the crowd. Two soldiers fell dead. A third was struck in the head with a heavy missile, dying as he collapsed on to the street. An uncontrollable and raging mob beat a fourth soldier to death. On this day, the first drops of blood in a battle of the one-week-old Civil War were spilled along the streets of Baltimore. What occurred on this day would always be known as the Pratt Street Riot. Later in the day, when Marylanders were called to defend their state against the incursion of Northern troops, their action would be called the "Lexington of 1861." The South always called it the "Battle of Baltimore."

CHAPTER I

Baltimore on the Eve of the Pratt Street Riot

April 1, 1861

To use the Bible to support slavery is analogous to using the Bible to support polygamy or other outmoded practices.
—*Rabbi David Einhorn, Congregation Har Sinai, Baltimore, April 1, 1861*

Baltimore was Maryland's major city before the Civil War. It was America's fourth-largest city (some historians say the third) with a population of 212,000. Like many important seaports, the city was home to a diverse mix of people. Baltimore's busy harbor, known as "the Basin," curled along the Patapsco River, which emptied into the northern end of the Chesapeake Bay. Baltimore's location, to the south and west of New York and Philadelphia, placed foreign imports and the city's manufactured products closer and more accessible to the western markets of Virginia, western Pennsylvania and Ohio and to Southern states as far south as Florida.

Baltimore's harbor bustled with maritime trade. Brawny stevedores and vans drawn by horses and carters hauled tons of commercial cargo along the city's docks, piers, warehouses and sheds. The white sails and the bare, furled masts of scores of tall wooden sailing ships could be seen from Pratt and Lombard Streets, important commercial thoroughfares running east and west through the city's downtown area parallel to the docks. A rail line ran along Pratt Street. It had been laid down to allow railway cars, pulled by horses, to connect the President Street Station and other depots in the city to the Baltimore and Ohio's (B&O) Camden Station. That station was the city's only departure point to the South. It was located on the southwest side of Baltimore.

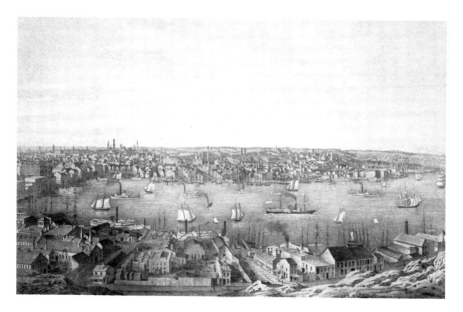

A view of Baltimore Harbor from Federal Hill. *Courtesy of Enoch Pratt Free Library, Maryland's State Resource Center, Baltimore, MD.*

Baltimore was also the South's largest city, since it was located forty miles below the Mason-Dixon line, the imaginary line America accepted as the geographic, cultural and political division between the North and the South. Baltimore was so close to the North, however, that it gave rise to the well-known saw that "Baltimore is the northernmost Southern city and the southernmost Northern city." The city may have been Southern, as it was located in a slave state, but its varied climate resembled that of its Mid-Atlantic neighbors—Philadelphia, Trenton and New York—with snow and frigid winters. Yet Baltimore's summers were also hot and humid like its steamier Southern sister cities of Savannah, Charleston and New Orleans. Trees and flowers that grew only in the North grew in Baltimore, and trees and flowers thriving only in the South could also be found there. Even the distinct Baltimore accent could be ascribed to neither the South nor the North. Maryland's citizens were divided on the issues of slavery, states rights and secession, the same rifts that split the North from the South.

As were Kentucky, Tennessee, Missouri and Delaware, Maryland was a border state, politically and geographically wedged between North and South. All the border states had populations that, like Maryland's, were divided on issues of slavery and states' rights. Maryland was home to 90,000 slaves, yet Baltimore, its largest city, counted only 2,118 men and women in bondage. Baltimore also hosted about 25,000 free blacks, the largest community of its type in the United States. These freedmen were an important part of the city's workforce.

Baltimore's citizens were politically and emotionally divided between pro- and anti-South and slavery. There were clashes as passions ran high about these issues and the right of a state to secede from the Union.

One religious leader, Rabbi David Einhorn, received threats for his long, outspoken and impassioned antislavery stand. While he would not yield to threats—even after the office of his antislavery newspaper, the *Sinai*, was destroyed—he was eventually forced to move to Philadelphia to ensure his family's safety. Union soldiers told him that he and his family were in danger because of his antislavery position. Within a month after the Pratt Street Riot, Einhorn was escorted out of the city under guard and on his way to Philadelphia. In contrast, Einhorn's colleague, Rabbi Bernard Illowy, left Baltimore to take up a pulpit in New Orleans, where he felt more comfortable with his new proslavery congregation. The problem was not limited to the Jewish community. A Lutheran minister's loyalty was questioned by the military because in a Sunday sermon he questioned the necessity of killing Southerners.

After Lincoln's election in 1860, many Marylanders clearly intended to try to force the state to secede from the Union. Of the almost 90,000 presidential ballots cast in Maryland among the four candidates (Abraham Lincoln, John Breckenridge, John Bell and Stephen Douglas), Lincoln limped in a poor last with only 2,294 votes. Breckenridge, the proslavery candidate, garnered the largest number of votes: 42,497. Lincoln was not well thought of in Maryland.

Despite the state's pro-Southern orientation, Maryland's governor, Thomas Hicks, was a sometime pro-Union member of the American Native Party, also called the Know-Nothings. After Lincoln's election and the secession of the Southern states, Hicks was under great pressure by his pro-South legislators to call a special session of the legislature. They wanted to fix Maryland's position on the issue of secession. He was holding them at bay, but he knew he would soon have to yield to them. Aside from its strategic location with respect to the nation's capital at Washington, should there be a war, Baltimore's industry would be vital to an agrarian South. Secessionists wanted to move this important prize into the Confederate corner.

By April, 1, 1861, seven states, rejecting Lincoln as their president, broke away from the Union (South Carolina, Georgia, Florida, Alabama, Mississippi, Texas and Louisiana). They assumed the name Confederate States of America (CSA), electing Jefferson Davis, a West Point graduate, one-time secretary of war and most recently a resigned United States

A threatened Rabbi David Einhorn leaves Baltimore with his family. *Courtesy of the Jewish Museum of Maryland.*

senator from Mississippi, as their president. At political rallies, in newspaper editorials and at street corner meetings held all over Baltimore, people debated the possibility of Maryland breaking away from the Union. The troubled city was poised to see what its closest Southern neighbor, Virginia, which had yet to act, would do. Whose side would she choose?

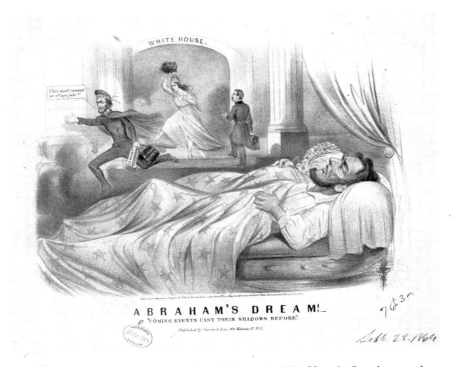

Lincoln dreams of his stealthy entrance into Baltimore in 1861. Note the Scotch cap and cloak he used as a disguise. *Courtesy Library of Congress.*

Baltimore was also the birthplace and an important center of America's commercial railroading. The Baltimore and Ohio Railroad (B&O) was the first in America to carry passengers for hire. The B&O had an important economic impact on the city as its rail systems ran in all directions out of the city. Its main depot at Camden Station, built in 1856, was the sole rail link to the nation's capital. Despite the importance of the B&O and the several other railroads that also serviced the city, the Baltimore City Council passed an ordinance in 1831 forbidding steam engines to operate within city limits. Trains running into Baltimore's many stations located around town required passengers to detrain and take horse-drawn cars along the Pratt Street rails to Camden Station. This law would play an important role in the Pratt Street Riot developing into such a bloody mêlée.

There was a brisk shipbuilding industry, and the city was an important center for the manufacture of flour and the heavy sailcloth used for sailing ships. Many of the manufacturing facilities were powered by mills along the banks of the Jones Falls, a river running into the city and emptying into

The Jones Falls, looking south, running into Baltimore Harbor. Note the factories. *Courtesy of Enoch Pratt Free Library, Maryland's State Resource, Baltimore MD.*

the Patapsco River. Fishing ships made their way to Baltimore from the Chesapeake Bay, sailing up the Patapsco and unloading heaps of fresh fish, crabs, oysters and other seafood. Their catches were destined for the city's tables and those of surrounding communities.

Dominating the busy, downtown commercial corner of Baltimore and South Streets was a large and modern architectural wonder, the five-story Sun Iron Building. It was designed by pioneer architect James Bogardus, a leading exponent of cast-iron façade buildings. The structure was the first of America's tall buildings using cast iron for structural support. Completed in 1851, it was home to the *Sun*, one of the city's leading newspapers, which, while pro-South, was not an advocate of secession. The building held everyone's attention from its first day. Designed with innovative arches and vaulted arcades, the radical design changed the face of the city's business district in the decade since its completion. Office buildings and factories of similar design were sprinkled throughout downtown Baltimore. But it was the Sun Iron Building that tourists and students of architecture came to gaze upon with awe and academic appreciation. Along the outside of the building's second floor, Bogardus placed two large, iron plaques depicting Benjamin Franklin and George Washington, both of whom looked out upon the citizens of this busy city.

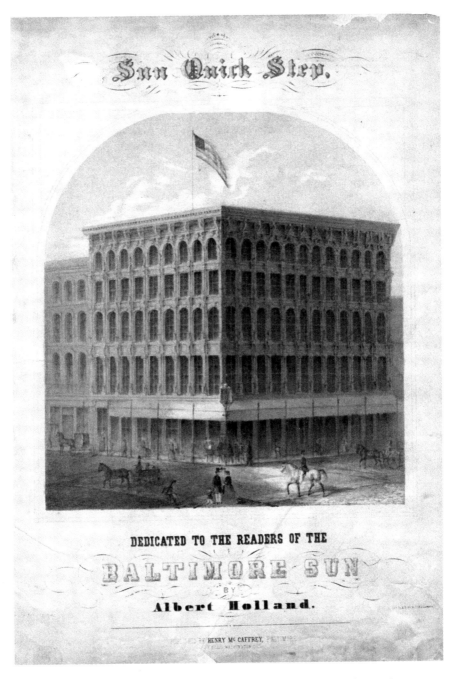

The innovative Sun Iron Building at the corner of Baltimore and South Streets, just steps from Pratt Street. *Courtesy Enoch Pratt Free Library, Maryland's State Resource Center, Baltimore, MD.*

The sitting chief justice of the United States Supreme Court, Roger B. Taney, who would play a historic role in the Pratt Street Riot, was a Marylander and a former slave owner who once lived in Baltimore. Much of his popularity among Southerners was based on his 1857 decision in the Dred Scott case. In this opinion, Taney held that slaves could not be American citizens, had no standing to sue in the federal courts and could not be taken away from their owners or become free merely because they resided in a nonslave state. Taney was the brother-in-law and former law partner of Francis Scott Key, the distinguished Baltimorean who wrote "The Star Spangled Banner." During the naval War of 1812, at the Battle of Baltimore, Key happened to be aboard a British warship anchored off Fort McHenry. He was on a government errand negotiating the exchange of prisoners of war. When the sun rose after a fierce nighttime battle, he saw the American flag still flying above Fort McHenry. It inspired him to write what became America's national anthem.

Fort McHenry itself was an important reminder to Baltimoreans and the rest of the nation of how, in this city, a young and raw country stood firm against one of the world's most powerful military machines. For it was here that ordinary citizens fought alongside soldiers, avenging America's honor. Together they beat back the British invaders who had, shortly before assaulting Baltimore, torched the White House to the country's humiliation. The proud city erected a monument to that victory called the "Battle Monument." It stood in Monument Square, an important social and political section of the city.

The statue of Justice Roger Taney in Mt. Vernon Square. Under his left arm rests the Constitution. *Photo courtesy of Marcus Dagan.*

Every large city along the Atlantic seaboard was home to immigrants, and Baltimore was no exception. After New York and Boston, Baltimore was the third most popular port of entry for Europe's immigrants.

The Battle Monument commemorating the Battle of Baltimore, 1814. *Courtesy of Enoch Pratt Free Library, Maryland's State Resource Center, Baltimore, MD.*

The Irish settled mainly in the poor southwest section of the city, close to the B&O railroad facilities, where many of the lucky ones found work. Germans also found homes throughout the city when they were driven from their country by the religious divisions and the political upheavals of the Revolution of 1848.

Among some of the city's prominent landmarks were Federal Hill, Washington Monument and the Phoenix Shot Tower. Federal Hill, a promontory located on the south side of the harbor, was in a working-class neighborhood. From the top of the hill, there were stunning views of the harbor and Baltimore's business district. From Federal Hill, one could also look out to the northern edges of the city's limits and see America's first monument dedicated to George Washington. Completed in 1829, the monument rose on the crest of a ridge in the city's Mt. Vernon district, where handsome nineteenth-century mansions and brownstones of the well-to-do lined the lovely neighborhood's quiet streets. The marble spire is topped with a statue of George Washington, who does not wear his military uniform but is wrapped within a classic, flowing Roman toga. In 1861, when Baltimore's homes and commercial buildings were uniformly low, sailors and passengers aboard ships entering the harbor could look a mile up the rise at Charles Street, one of the city's great avenues, and see America's first president standing atop his gleaming white monument.

In 1861, the Phoenix Shot Tower, constructed of one million red bricks and reaching a height of 234 feet, was America's tallest structure. Built in 1828, it was still being used commercially. Pistol and rifle shot were manufactured there by dropping molten lead from the top of the tower into a sieve. The hot liquid lead traveled all the way down the tall tower into a vat of cold water, finishing up as pellets destined for use as pistol and rifle balls.

The city was also home to notorious gangs with colorful names like the Plug Uglies, the Riff Raffs, the American Rattlers and the Blood Tubs. The Blood Tubs were said to have earned that name by dipping their victims into tubs filled with animal blood. The gangs, whose prominence gave rise to the name "Mob Town," were especially active at election time. They kidnapped voters, holding them for days; broke up political rallies; and caused general mayhem. Some commentators have speculated that writer Edgar Allan Poe may have been kidnapped by one of these gangs during an election, filled with liquor and dragged to several polling stations around town so he could cast multiple votes. Finished with him, gang members dumped him on the street, sick and unconscious, leaving him to die.

Baltimore had a long and dark history with respect to mobs. During the 1830s, mobs reacted to bank failures by rioting against the banks and their executives for more than two days in what was known as the "Bank Riots." At Monument Square, citizen volunteers and police had to fire into an uncontrollable crowd. The U.S. Army also had to be called in to help quell the riots. Public disturbances were still a regular feature of life in the city, until a new mayor, George Brown, was elected in 1860 on his promise to rid Baltimore of violence and the freewheeling mobs that ran throughout the city. Brown was also to play an important role in the Pratt Street Riot.

This was the city of Baltimore on the eve of the Civil War and the Pratt Street Riot—a bustling city, an important sea, rail and manufacturing center, where pro- and anti-Southerners, slaves, freedmen, immigrants and street gangs mingled with one another. It was also home to a politically divided population, probably more oriented to the South than the North. And, as was the rest of the South after Abraham Lincoln's recent election, it was waiting for something to happen.

CHAPTER II

A Prelude to Baltimore's Bloody Riot

April 12, 1861, Fort Sumter, Charleston, South Carolina

Nobody has been hurt after all. How gay we were last night. Reaction after the dread of all the slaughter we thought those dreadful cannon were making. Not even a battery the worse for wear... he [Major Anderson] *has not yet silenced any of our guns.*
—Entry in Mary Chesnut's diary after the Battle of Fort Sumter

South Carolina, the first state to secede from the Union, wanted Fort Sumter for its own. It took the logical position that since that federal facility was inside the new nation's territory, it now belonged to the Confederate States of America (CSA) and should be ceded for the use of the fledgling country. After all, Fort Sumter guarded the entrance to Charleston Harbor and, more important, to the city itself. It would not do to have another country control this fort in such a strategic location. Governor Francis Pickens of South Carolina demanded it be surrendered at once.

Before Governor Pickens made his formal demand, Major Robert Anderson, commander of all the forts in Charleston Harbor, sensed that his position at Fort Moultrie in the harbor was untenable. Major Anderson evacuated Moultrie on December 26, 1860, moving his men and equipment over to Fort Sumter, which at the time had not yet been finished and lacked a garrison. Anderson then set out to fortify his position. Governor Pickens advised Anderson that this was a hostile act, as South Carolina had been negotiating with the federal government to take over all federal facilities in that state.

At first there were polite notes and formal negotiations passing back and forth between the opponents. All the while, the South Carolinians were taking over the nearby forts—Moultrie, Pinckney and Johnson—all of which had been effectively abandoned by Anderson. Pickens ordered them garrisoned and equipped with cannons, mortars and other heavy armaments. All were aimed at Fort Sumter.

Anderson tried bringing in additional supplies to Fort Sumter. President Lincoln sent the merchant vessel *Star of the West*, laden with food, ammunition and additional troops. As the *Star of the West* approached Fort Sumter, it was warned not to sail on with an unfriendly Confederate shot placed close across its bow. The vessel proceeded, but after being directly fired upon, the *Star of the West* retreated. Its cargo never reached Fort Sumter.

When all the notes and, later, direct negotiations failed, P.G.T. Beauregard, lately superintendent of West Point Academy and now a newly commissioned Confederate general, was sent to Charleston by CSA president Jefferson Davis. His orders were to capture the fort. Major Anderson had once been Beauregard's artillery instructor at West Point.

During the early morning hours of April 12, 1861, after all the polite notes and civil face-to-face negotiations had failed, Beauregard ordered his Confederate artillery to open fire on the fort. Southern artillerymen showered thousands of deadly mortar and cannon shells, ranging from eight to thirty-six pounds, from their positions at Fort Moultrie on Sullivan's Island, as well as other locations surrounding Fort Sumter. After holding back, Anderson finally answered the fire. The battle for Fort Sumter had begun and was the first open clash between the North and the South in the Civil War.

The hostilities lasted thirty-four hours. After the battle, Anderson filed a report with Simon Cameron, Lincoln's secretary of war. It was obvious that the defenders had suffered the worst of the battle. Major Anderson's student had learned his artillery lessons well. Anderson reported that the quarters at Fort Sumter were entirely consumed by flames. The main gates were destroyed; the magazine was aflame and its doors warped and jammed from intense heat. Anderson was left with four barrels and three cartridges of powder. All the food was gone except for some pork.

In contrast, Anderson could report that only Fort Moultrie's interior buildings were destroyed. Despite all the destruction, politeness and civility continued to prevail. Correct notes passed between the enemies detailing how the Confederate takeover of Fort Sumter would occur and how the Union forces would evacuate the fort.

Despite the thousands of shells passing between the combatants, neither side recorded a casualty, due in part to Anderson's refusal to answer fire at the onset of hostilities. Two Union soldiers did die, however, and two more were wounded through an unfortunate accident. After Anderson surrendered the fort, Beauregard graciously allowed him to fire a one-hundred-gun salute to the American flag. As the flag was being lowered during the salute, a magazine with gunpowder used to fire off the tribute accidentally exploded before it reached fifty guns, causing the casualties. The tribute was then prudently reduced to fifty guns.

On April 15, the day after Major Anderson ceded Fort Sumter to General Beauregard, President Lincoln issued an urgent call to the nation in a proclamation. In the first paragraph, Lincoln admitted that the government lacked enough power to force the seceding states back into the Union. He said, "The laws of the United States have for some time past and now are opposed…in the states of South Carolina, Georgia, Alabama, Florida, Mississippi, Louisiana and Texas by combinations too powerful to be suppressed…by judicial proceedings or by the powers vested in the Marshals by law."

Lincoln then called for the militia of the various states to volunteer their services so that he, as president, could restore order:

> *I…hereby call forth a Militia of the several states of the Union to the number of Seventy five thousand, in order to suppress said combinations* [the seceding states] *and to cause the laws to be duly executed.*

At the same time, Lincoln convened both Houses of Congress in this proclamation so that they might deal with the crisis. On April 17, Virginia, in defiance of Lincoln's call and after much debate by its legislature, finally declared it would throw in with the Confederacy and formally seceded from the Union.

The hostilities at Fort Sumter started the Civil War, but death and the blood of battle had yet to flow. The news of the fall of Fort Sumter was first received in Baltimore at the telegraph office of the B&O's Camden Street Station.

CHAPTER III

Trying to Prevent a Riot

April 15 to April 18, 1861

There was a deep and pervading impression of impending evil. And now an immediate fear was as to the effect on the citizens of the passage of Northern troops through the city.
—George William Brown, mayor of Baltimore

Lincoln's call for volunteers on April 15 greatly troubled Baltimore's civic leaders and politicians. They knew the only way soldiers could get to Washington was to pass through their city. They also knew that because of the law requiring rail transfers from one terminal to another within the city of Baltimore, soldiers would have to openly move through the streets. The sight of Union soldiers standing out in their blue uniforms, traveling from different depots around the city to Camden Station, would certainly inflame the public. The idea that these soldiers were heading south for a possible invasion of the Confederate states, they argued, could set off anti-Union demonstrations or worse: a serious riot.

Already anticipating trouble on April 16, the day before Virginia's decision to secede from the Union, Baltimore's police chief, George P. Kane, a staunch and outspoken secessionist, learned that troops answering Lincoln's call for volunteers would be passing through his city. Without consulting with Baltimore's mayor or Maryland's governor, Chief Kane sent the following message to William Crawford, the Baltimore agent of the Philadelphia, Wilmington and Baltimore Railroad (PW&B), the line that he learned would be transporting military units from the North:

Dear Sir:

Is it true as stated that an attempt will be made to pass the volunteers from New York intended to war upon the South over your road today? It is important that we have explicit understanding on that subject.

Your friend, George P. Kane

On April 17, Mayor George Brown, also aware that there might be trouble, issued his own proclamation. He asked the citizens of Baltimore to remain calm and refrain from "harshness of speech." Simon Cameron, Lincoln's secretary of war, sent Maryland's governor, Thomas Hicks, a communication dated April 18, 1861, warning Hicks not to prevent Union troops from entering Baltimore. Everyone in a position of responsibility was aware that there would be trouble. On April 18, news of troop movements through Baltimore was received from Pennsylvania. The city could expect two artillery companies and four companies of Pennsylvania state militia to arrive on that day. They would be arriving at the Bolton Street Station on the Northern Central Railroad.

Only the artillerymen, who were regular army, wore uniforms. They were detailed on to Fort McHenry. The Pennsylvania militiamen, who wore civilian clothes, mostly lacked weapons. They were to go on to Washington. Accounts indicate that only the militiamen were booed and taunted as they were being transferred to Camden Station.

Bird's-eye view of Baltimore. Camden Station is at the left and President Station is to the right of the harbor. *Courtesy Library of Congress.*

Police Chief Kane was at Bolton Street awaiting their arrival and ready to give the men protection as they marched through Baltimore's streets (apparently, they would not be using horsecars to transfer). Kane's cadre of police officers was placed on either side of the marchers as they proceeded, preventing violence for the most part. Stones were thrown at the Pennsylvanians, and the Afro-American servant of one of the officers, Nicholas Biddle, was struck on the head, the first Union casualty after Fort Sumter. Nevertheless, the extent of the crowd's abuse was verbal, and the artillerymen and the militia arrived at their destinations safely. The Pennsylvanians were surprised at their reception.

On the same day, the Sixth Massachusetts, also answering the call for volunteers to defend the Union, was marching triumphantly to cheers on its way to the train station in New York City. The Sixth was scheduled to get to Baltimore the next day. The men would arrive at the President Street Station in the morning, change trains and proceed on a Baltimore and Ohio (B&O) train to Washington. Unlike the Pennsylvania volunteers, the Sixth's soldiers were clad in uniforms and carried weapons. The Sixth even brought its brigade band with it. The *New York Times* noted the presence of the Massachusetts volunteers and their cheering reception in an article titled "Enlistment Is for the War." The Sixth Massachusetts was proud of being the first to answer President Lincoln's call for assistance, just as its minutemen ancestors had done almost a century earlier. The minutemen were the first to fight the British in the Revolutionary War, and these volunteers of the Sixth came from some of the same towns, such as Groton, Acton and Lowell.

On the morning of the eighteenth, a group calling itself the States' Rights Convention met at Taylor's Building at Fayette and Calvert Streets. They were, for the most part, well-respected members of the city and took the position that there should no longer be any troop movements through the city. The meeting was later characterized by an attendee as an "excited secession meeting." On the same day, Governor Hicks met with Mayor Brown and showed him a proclamation he had also prepared in which he called for Baltimoreans not to be rash and remain calm. He also advised Marylanders that he would send no soldiers from their state except to defend the capital.

There was no doubt that by now most Baltimoreans were aware that soldiers would be passing through their city and state, coming here from Massachusetts and arriving on the nineteenth. They even knew they would be pulling in at the President Street Station. Some of the citizens of Baltimore were ready to meet them to show their displeasure at the use of their city to transit troops that would be fighting against the South. What happened next should have been no surprise.

CHAPTER IV

A Plan to Assassinate Lincoln

A feeling of indignation that Mr. Lincoln, who was no coward, but proved himself on many occasions to be a brave man, was prevented [by others]...from journeying to Baltimore in the light of day, in the company of his wife and children, relying...on the honor and manhood of the American people.
—*George W. Brown, mayor of Baltimore, 1860–62*

A series of unfortunate events joined together to create the Pratt Street Riot. First, the thirty-year-old ordinance forbidding the operation of steam engines in the city obliged the Union troops on both the eighteenth and nineteenth to transfer from their terminating depots on their way to Camden Station, where trains to Washington awaited them. The forced transfer made the soldiers of the Sixth Massachusetts vulnerable as, unlike the Pennsylvanians a day earlier, they had to stop and wait while horsecars hitched up and then rolled over Pratt Street's rails to Camden Station. The troops would have to move along one of the city's main thoroughfares, dressed in uniforms, carrying rifles and in full view of an angry and divided population. It would be considered a Northern invasion of their city by many who were sympathetic to the South.

But for the ordinance forbidding steam locomotives in the city's limits, the soldiers would have passed through the city or its outskirts, where, traveling at full speed, they would have been safer. Finally, the city's history of creating rowdy crowd actions, together with the presence of active pro-secessionists now fueled by the fall of Fort Sumter and Virginia's recent secession, all joined together to act as catalysts for the Pratt Street Riot and the first deaths and casualties resulting in battle of the Civil War.

An earlier incident in the city also added to the anger and distaste many Baltimoreans felt about anything Northern. It left them with a bad memory of their new president.

In February 1861, President Lincoln left Springfield, Illinois, en route to Washington for his inauguration. At that time, presidential inaugurations were held on March 11. Lincoln planned to make several stops along the way to meet with his new constituents. As would the Sixth Massachusetts Volunteers two months later, Lincoln also traveled on a train belonging to the PW&B. Arriving at Baltimore for one of his advertised stops, his train was scheduled to pull in at the Calvert Street Station. An announcement was made that he would arrive late on the morning of February 23. Lincoln's train also had to make a city transfer. But as well-wishers, including the city's mayor, George Brown, gathered at the station to greet the new president, they were disappointed. When the train arrived, only Mrs. Lincoln and her three children emerged.

Lincoln had secretly preceded his family hours earlier, boarding the PW&B at Harrisburg at 11:00 p.m. and arriving at Baltimore after a stop at Philadelphia, during the quiet hour of 3:30 a.m. Upon the advice of his security guards, the president followed this travel precaution to foil what was believed to be an assassination plot. At Harrisburg, Lincoln was advised to substitute his trademark stovepipe hat for a softer and smaller Scotch tam-o'-shanter and to wear his coat and a shawl draped over his shoulders to reduce his distinctive height. At Philadelphia, Lincoln changed trains

Washington Monument at Mt. Vernon, looking toward the harbor. On the left is Calvert Station, which Lincoln used in stealth in 1861. *Courtesy Enoch Pratt Free Library, Maryland's State Resource Center, Baltimore, MD.*

and was escorted into a sleeping car reserved for invalids. All telegraph communications were suspended as Lincoln's train proceeded on. Colonel Charles Sumner, one of Lincoln's party, called it a "damned piece of cowardice." He advised the president to travel openly and with a cavalry guard to accompany him to Washington. His advice was ignored.

It was a decision Lincoln would later publicly regret. He followed the advice of the Pinkerton National Detective Agency. They were private detectives from Chicago led by Allen Pinkerton. Hired by Lincoln to act as his security guards, as the federal government did not provide presidents complete protection at the time, Lincoln relied on their judgment. The detectives who would become known simply as "the Pinkertons" claimed to have uncovered what was a supposed plot, planned in Baltimore, to assassinate Lincoln and disrupt the inauguration. The Pinkertons even implicated Police Chief Kane, describing him as an openly avowed secessionist and a person who would be pleased to see Lincoln out of the way. Historians later doubted that there was ever such a plot, and certainly there was never any proof that Kane conspired in any way to harm Lincoln. Yet even the *New York Times* was impressed with the story, commenting on such a possible assassination in its February 23 edition. Among the alleged conspirators the Pinkertons uncovered was a dissident group calling itself the Baltimore Society of the Knights of Liberty. Pinkertons arrested some of the members of this pro-Southern group, which then dissolved, its other members disappearing into the city.

A shadowy and alleged participant in the plot was Cipriano Ferrandini, a Corsican immigrant who ran a barbershop in the basement of Barnum's Hotel. The hotel, one of the city's finest, was also a favorite gathering place for Southern sympathizers and smugglers. John Wilkes Booth, Lincoln's assassin in 1865, regularly frequented the hotel. There has been much speculation about whether Ferrandini and Booth actually met and engaged in any conspiracy at Barnum's. An opera by Hollis Thoms, called *The Moustache*, was based on such speculation.

On January 26, 1861, a resolution passed Congress to investigate whether "any secret organizations hostile to the United States existed." As far back as eleven days before Lincoln's March inauguration (two months before the Pratt Street Riot), Ferrandini, who was frank, open and notorious in his anti-Union remarks, was summoned to appear before a congressional committee investigating attempts to disrupt the inauguration and perhaps even harm Lincoln. Ferrandini freely admitted his attachment to the South. Even at this early date, he told the congressmen that he was resolved to keep Union troops from going through Baltimore on their way to wage war against the

South. Ferrandini however, denied any attempt to harm the president or disrupt the inauguration. He had however, acquired military training in Mexico, sponsored by secessionists, returning to Baltimore with the rank of captain; thereafter, he was often addressed with that rank.

Pinkerton agents claimed to have met with Ferrandini at a hotel, and then later at a bar, where he informed them that "Lincoln must surely die." Despite his open testimony before the congressional committee, Ferrandini was not arrested until a year later and was then quickly released. When Maryland's Governor Hicks appeared before the same committee investigating threats to Lincoln, he told the legislators that he thought there was a plot to assassinate Lincoln but that it no longer existed.

With the testimonies of Hicks and Ferrandini, the presence of Baltimore's large pro-Southern population and the city's past history of mob action, federal authorities certainly had enough information and good reason to anticipate problems with safety associated with any troop movements through Baltimore. All this was known much before April 19. Why the authorities never thought to use alternative routes or provide protection for the troops has never been established.

George Brown, Baltimore's mayor at the time, writing in his memoir, *Baltimore & the Nineteenth of April, 1861*, raises this very issue. He maintained that if the troops had marched together as an armed unit through the city to Camden Station, accompanied by Baltimore police as a backup, instead of clumsily transferring to railway cars, they could have done so in safety. Brown also faults the PW&B for failing to notify the city exactly when the troops were scheduled to arrive so that proper arrangements could be made with the police for their safety.

Then there was the unfortunate result of Lincoln's secret ride through their city, an event that angered many Baltimoreans. The city had already received too much unwanted publicity as a place filled with roughs and home to a nest of violent conspirators. The news spread nationally that a group of assassins in Baltimore was waiting to get at the president and disrupt the inauguration ceremonies. Lincoln having to "sneak" through the city for his personal safety called up more nasty images throughout America of Baltimore as a violent and dangerous place, deserving of its name: "Mob Town." Baltimore was outraged and angry.

As for Lincoln, because he snuck through the city, he was now perceived by many—especially his political enemies, Southerners and Baltimoreans—as a coward. Newspaper cartoons portrayed him riding through Baltimore disguised in women's clothes or peeking warily and in fear through a half-opened door as if reluctant to step outside.

CHAPTER V

The Civil War's First Blood

Pratt Street, Baltimore, April 19, 1861

In the opinion of this convention the massing of large bodies of militia, exclusively from the free States, in the District of Columbia, is uncalled for…[and] *is a menace to the State of Maryland, and an insult to her loyalty and good will.*
—Resolution of the States' Rights Convention, Baltimore, April 18, 1861

The first drops of Civil War blood, resulting more from angry and violent confrontation than from a formal battle between two armies, were spilled along the streets of Baltimore. On that day, April 19, 1861, the Civil War came closer to developing into the tragic conflict between America's brothers, sons and friends. The deaths and wounds suffered along Pratt Street occurred one week after the war's first cannon shots were fired on Fort Sumter, six hundred miles distant. Since the first day of battle in South Carolina, there had been no other serious encounters between the North and South.

The mêlée known as the Pratt Street Riot would change all that and the face of Baltimore for years to come. It placed the city under tight military control for the remainder of the Civil War. Baltimore became a city to be watched and controlled, a city upon which strong force would be swiftly exerted if needed.

On April 19, 1861, four Union soldiers were killed and thirty-six wounded. Civilians suffered twelve deaths. The number of civilian wounded remains unknown to this day, as many of the rioters melted into the city, disappearing after being pursued by police, who were called in to break up the riot.

Early on the morning of the nineteenth, as the Sixth Massachusetts Volunteers left the station at Philadelphia on their way to Washington, their commander, Colonel Edward F. Jones, received an urgent telegraph message. It came from Baltimore and advised him that an angry mob of Southern sympathizers awaited his men at the President Street Station. Jones was surprised. This was very different from the positive greetings his men had received at every stop on their trip south. Throughout New Jersey and Pennsylvania, they were greeted as heroes. A day earlier, these same troops had been greeted with cheers and applause as they marched smartly through the streets of New York City on their way to the railroad station on one of their stops taking them to Washington. And the *New York Times* noted their presence in a positive article titled "Enlistment Is for the War."

But on the eighteenth, the same day Jones's Sixth Massachusetts Volunteers were being received warmly in New York, Baltimoreans had refused to extend a similar welcome to a contingent of Pennsylvania volunteers passing through their city to Camden Yards from Bolton Station. Jones was informed that those soldiers, some of whom were destined for Washington and others to Baltimore's Fort McHenry, marched through the city safely. Yet there was an ominous show of anger, jeers, taunts and much verbal abuse, including occasional missiles hurled at the Pennsylvanians by a crowd that had collected along the route to Camden Station. The soldiers needed a police escort to march on to Camden Station, because only half of the group was armed. Jones didn't know it at the time, but one of the Pennsylvania soldiers later described their angry greeting as being "surrounded by a hooting, yelling crowd, who lavished the most opprobrious epithets upon us."

Colonel Jones was impressed with the urgency of the message, as he was responsible for the safety of the men under his command. His volunteers were divided into a dozen companies, each led by an officer. In his report detailing the Pratt Street Riot to the War Department, prepared on April 22, Jones made the following comments:

> *After leaving Philadelphia, I received intimation that the passage through the city of Baltimore would be resisted. I caused ammunition to be distributed and arms loaded, and went personally through the cars and issued the following order viz;*
>
> *The regiment will march through Baltimore in columns of sections, arms at will. You will undoubtedly be insulted, abused and perhaps assaulted, to which you must pay no attention whatever, but march to the front and pay no attention to the mob, even if they throw stones, bricks or other missiles; but if you are fired upon, and any of you are hit, your officers will order you*

*to fire. Do not fire into any promiscuous crowds, but drop any man whom
you might see aiming at you and be sure you drop him.*

Obviously, Jones did not have much time to plan for the hostile crowd
he now knew would soon be awaiting him at President Station. He did the
best he could. He had no way of knowing that it would soon turn into an
uncontrollable riot. Nevertheless, as a good commander, he prepared his
men for the worst.

There was a change of procedure, however, that would also play an
important factor in the birth of the riot. Instead of marching as a unified
force, as had been planned earlier, it was decided to have the troops remain
in their railway cars, each of which it was determined would now be pulled
by teams of four horses galloping at top speed on Pratt Street's rails through
the city.

As they proceeded to Baltimore, Jones entered into the cars to prepare
his men for trouble. He found them in good spirits. They were singing, but
they turned serious when Jones alerted them about what they could expect
at Baltimore. Aside from the preparation, Jones ordered ten rounds of
ammunition distributed to every soldier.

On the same train accompanying Colonel Jones's Sixth Massachusetts,
was the Twenty-sixth Pennsylvania, a group of twelve hundred volunteers
led by Colonel William F. Small. Unlike the Sixth, the Pennsylvanians
were unarmed.

At ten thirty that morning, between thirty-one and thirty-four horse-
drawn cars rolling over Pratt Street's railroad tracks had already been
assembled to move the almost two thousand soldiers, including a regimental
band and all their baggage, in railway cars from the President Street Station
to Camden Station. Soon after their arrival at Baltimore, several companies
of Massachusetts volunteers were already hooking up to the first of nine cars
that would carry them on their way to Camden Station. As they trundled
along in the railway cars, the soldiers were accompanied by a pressing and
milling crowd of angry, but as yet not large nor physically aggressive, civilians
following alongside. The first cars in this caravan turned from President on
to Pratt Street on the way to their destination. At Pratt Street, the mob had
grown and became more menacing. It had been swelling for some time, and
now it pushed dangerously close to the soldiers. The tracks over the bridge
at the Jones Falls near Concord and Pratt Streets were blocked. They had
been covered with tools and equipment. Eight cars in the caravan led by
Colonel Jones had gotten through, but the ninth and last car in the caravan

Note the rail and horse carriages on Pratt Street. This is the route soldiers took marching from President Street, at right, to Camden, at left. *Courtesy of Library of Congress, Geography and Map Division.*

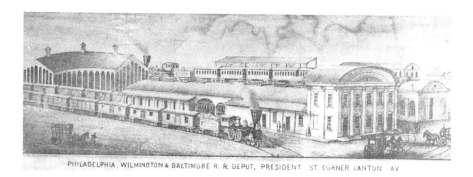

PHILADELPHIA, WILMINGTON & BALTIMORE R. R. DEPOT, PRESIDENT ST. CORNER CANTON AV

President Street. Note the rails on the street used for transfers to Camden Station. Large rail sheds extend past the waiting room. *Courtesy Enoch Pratt Free Library, Maryland's State Resource Center, Baltimore, MD.*

was unable to pass and was forced to return to President Street. The first eight proceeded on along Pratt Street in the midst of what was becoming a howling and uncontrollable mob.

The last car, which was now returning to President Street, carried four companies, C, D, I and L, and the brigade band of Lowell, Massachusetts. They were led by Captain Albert S. Follansbee, the officer in charge of Company C, Lowell Mechanical Phalanx.

His four companies having tried unsuccessfully to follow their comrades, Captain Follansbee had the horses on his car rehitched and placed at the rear so that he could return to President Street. Twenty years later, one of the soldiers at a reunion of the Pratt Street Riot held in Baltimore recalled how he and his comrades were finally ordered out of their car. "Our Captain [Follansbee] said: 'Men file out. March as close as you possibly can. Fire on no man unless compelled.'"

Meanwhile, Colonel Small's Pennsylvanians were still at the station waiting for their transportation. Since they were unarmed and unable to defend themselves, Colonel Small was advised by Governor Hicks to return to Philadelphia. This group would be under continued attack at the President Street Station until the men boarded the returning train.

Colonel Jones, now on the farthest side of Pratt Street and on his way to Camden Station, learned that Follansbee had turned back. He issued the following order to Captain Follansbee, who had by now returned to President Street: "You will march to this place [Camden Station] as quick as possible [and] follow the railroad track." After receiving this order, Follansbee decided to leave the members of the brigade band at President Street to await further orders.

Later, the band members were also victims of attacks, along with the unarmed Pennsylvanians. Some band members ran into the city to hide after ripping off regimental stripes from their uniforms in an effort to blend in with the citizenry. By nighttime, they managed to find their way to police stations, where they were protected and were later able to rejoin their unit.

Proceeding as ordered by Colonel Jones, Follansbee and his men now marched up President Street on their second attempt to get to Camden Station. It would be over a mile and a half's march under the worst possible conditions, resulting in deaths and wounds for both the soldiers and their pursuing rioters. As the soldiers left the President Street Depot, they were seen cocking their rifles for ready firing. They had advanced just a few blocks under a shower of bottles, bricks, stones and verbal abuse when, at Fawn Street, they were besieged by a larger and angrier mob with other ideas. Rioters marched alongside the soldiers, mocking them and shouting praises to the South, to Jefferson Davis, to secession and to South Carolina.

One man marched before the soldiers carrying the palmetto standard of South Carolina, making it appear as if the Massachusetts men were soldiers of the South. Lieutenant Leander Lynde stepped out from behind his men and strode directly into the mob, grabbed the flag and tore it from its staff. Lynde then stuffed it under his tunic and returned to his men. A lone

The Sixth Massachusetts firing into the crowd. *Courtesy Enoch Pratt Free Library, Maryland's State Resource Center, Baltimore, MD.*

police officer joined up with the marching soldiers to guide them on to their destination. Both Lynde and the police officer exhibited great bravery before this uncontrollable and increasingly emotional crowd.

That day, laborers had been working on the roadway along Gay and Pratt Streets, and there were tools, sand, loose cobblestones and other equipment strewn about. Another mob, now collecting along Pratt Street, had already dealt with the first group of soldiers still in railway cars. They had piled sand and tools on the tracks, preventing their use and cutting off Follansbee and his men from their comrades, who were now again proceeding ahead. Some sympathetic sailors from nearby ships, seeing the swelling mob, dragged an anchor one block from the Gay Street dock and hauled it across the tracks. Along the same street, loose cobblestones, rocks, bottles and tools were now being hurled at one of the streetcars. It was the last of those that had preceded Follansbee's group. This car was under the command of Major Benjamin Watson, the last car of the now reduced eight-car caravan.

Follansbee and his men now advanced to the corner of Pratt and President Streets. When they turned left on Pratt, they were met by a wall of rioters assembled to prevent them from going on. The soldiers heard more loud shouts and taunts directed at them. As they approached the Jones

Falls Bridge, now several yards in front of them, they could see the mob ahead piling obstacles atop one another to blockade the rails running over the bridge.

Ahead of Follansbee, Major Watson, commanding the last car of the caravan that had continued on, was beginning to experience severe violence. Watson's car was suffering attacks with cobblestones, bottles and other missiles, many of which smashed windows and found their way against the sides of the railway car.

The mob was now growing uglier. Follansbee could see Major Watson's car. Trying to cross the bridge over the Jones Falls, Watson's progress was stalled when his car was derailed. Follansbee could see that the windows of the rail car were now smashed in and that the sides of the car were cratered with dents from the heavy cobblestones thrown in anger and rage. Missiles showered down on the car like huge, deadly hailstones.

Watson acted quickly. In order to continue moving and get back on the tracks, he commandeered a loose team of horses from a frightened conductor, who refused to help. Watson pulled his pistol out from his holster and threatened to shoot the shaking conductor in the head if he did not comply with the order. After returning the car to the tracks, Watson told his men to remain flat on the floor and not to use their weapons. When one of his men called out that he was wounded by gunfire, Watson ordered his men "to rise up from the floor and return fire."

Meanwhile, Follansbee and his men were out in the open, moving along Pratt Street and physically exposed to the crowd, while Watson's soldiers ahead of him were somewhat safer, still in their car. The crowd was getting more aggressive, and many more among the mob were now collecting paving stones, bottles and tools and hurling them at the soldiers in a deadly assault. Somehow, someone had even found a canoe to haul over the tracks. The rioters still cheered for Confederate president Jefferson Davis, the South and South Carolina. There were many loud calls for secession from the Union. Follansbee's marchers were moving along a wave of uncontrollable men shouting taunts at the soldiers, and now some of the rioters were firing shots into the air. Someone in the crowd finally aimed directly at the soldiers. Soldiers were wounded by bricks, bottles, tools and even bullets. The hapless volunteers were now moving at full speed, dragging their rifles, passing over the Jones Falls Bridge, picking their way across barriers made up of lumber, wire and even a cannon, which was aimed but not fired at them.

George Wilson Booth, one of the rioters, described the confusion and terror of that day.

A soldier, struck by a stone, fell almost at my feet, and as he fell, dropped his musket, which was immediately seized by Edward W. Beatty, a port customs officer, who raised it to his shoulder and fired into the column.

As he fired, he turned into the crowd and asked if anyone had a cartridge. I gave him one or two and showed him how to reload and then betook myself to the protection of the first doorway, thus escaping the bullets that were sweeping the street.

The rear files faced about and delivered a volley into the crowd, who responded with pistol shots, stones, clubs and other missiles. A perfect fusillade for the next few blocks was kept up by the troops and the outraged mob.

This extraordinary narrative deserves some comment. In the first place, within the mob there were obviously some responsible citizens. One writer, George L. Radcliffe, agrees. He notes that "many prominent and respectable persons were to be found in their ranks [the rioters], seeking to repel what they considered an invasion of Maryland."

Booth proceeds to tell his readers that he met a certain Mr. Beatty, whom he obviously knew and who was a federal customs officer, a somewhat responsible position that, at the time, was usually a political appointment. Later, as we shall see, another well-known Baltimore businessman would be the last fatal casualty of that desperate day. So the mob wasn't made up exclusively of roughs; there were also many well-known and responsible citizens of Baltimore among this screaming pack of demonstrators, including the neighborhood merchants.

Booth goes on to tell his readers that not only did he come to be at this riot armed with cartridges in his pockets, but he also gave some cartridges to Beatty and then instructed him in the weapon's loading. So neither Booth nor Beatty was acting as a mere bystander; they were active participants. Then Booth tells his readers how perilous the situation was by using some strong words to describe the action that day: "Bullets...were sweeping the street." The soldiers "delivered a volley into the crowd." Finally, Booth describes "a perfect fusillade for the next few blocks [that] was kept up by the troops and the outraged crowd."

It was a full-blown battle, with men on both sides dying and falling wounded by bullets, rocks and clubs. Yet the fight lacked the discipline one might expect on the field of battle between two uniformed and militarily trained enemies. The mob, completely out of control by the time it reached Light Street, beat one of Follansbee's men to death. Another soldier who died after being struck on the head by a stone, had earlier told one of his friends, "We shall have trouble today, and I shall never make it out alive. Promise me, if I fall, that my body will be sent home."

It was a conflict marked by confusion and chaos. As described by Booth, Follansbee's men did return controlled fire directly into the crowd, and several civilians fell; some were dead, others suffered wounds. Now someone in the crowd flew another standard; this time, the Stars and Bars of the Confederate flag. As happened on Fawn Street, someone jumped ahead of the line of soldiers, who then made it appear as if they were marching to Southern colors. Another man ran from the crowd and unsuccessfully tried to tear the American flag from a soldier carrying it on a flagstaff. Brown tells us that it was a young and well-respected attorney who suffered a serious leg wound for his efforts. At the time, it was thought he was dead, but he survived his injuries. Now another man ran out of the crowd and succeeded in wresting a soldier's warm and recently fired musket from him. He fired the weapon into the solid wall of soldiers until Mayor Brown, who at the time was standing nearby in the midst of the mêlée, took the rifle from him. Brown would later be accused of firing the musket himself into the line of troops and killing a soldier, a charge he vigorously denied.

People were running to and from shops and offices alerting friends and neighbors to the battle taking place on Pratt Street. One young attorney, McHenry Howard, ran out to the street. He was the grandson of Francis Scott Key; brother of Frank Key Howard, editor of a pro-Southern newspaper; and son of Charles Howard, president of the board of police commissioners. Someone told McHenry about the mischief on Pratt Street. Howard, a member of the Fifty-third Infantry of Maryland Militia, asked, "Do I have time to get my uniform?"

"Damn your uniform," was the reply. Howard met his brother Frank at Baltimore and Calvert Streets, where they ran to the U.S. Armory. There they sat with weapons at the ready and without their uniforms awaiting orders. Would they assist the Union soldiers to maintain order, or would they drive them back? No matter what, they were resolved not to harm their fellow citizens.

Mayor George Brown, who was called out of his law offices on St. Paul Street by an urgent message from Police Chief Kane, rushed to the scene by carriage, accompanied by some members of the police commission, to see what was happening. Brown first went to Camden Station, where things were relatively quiet. Colonel Jones had arrived unscathed and was waiting for the rest of his men, and so Brown thought the affair had ended as it had a day earlier, without any casualties. Then he got word of the battle raging on Pratt Street. Now on his way to link up with Follansbee's soldiers, Brown ran into five police officers at the Gay Street dock trying to remove the anchor that the sailors had earlier dragged across the rails. The mob was preventing them from their work. Brown stepped in, and the officers were finally allowed to remove the anchor.

Brown then continued east along Pratt Street, where he finally caught up with the Massachusetts volunteers near the Jones Falls Bridge. Here the soldiers had already picked their way, with much difficulty, through a formidable barrier of lumber and other equipment piled high and stacked across the roadway to prevent their advance. When Brown caught up with them, they had already broken through to other side of the barricade and were racing west down Pratt Street. He describes their pace as being so fast that they could not stop to take proper aim at the pursuing crowd. Brown bravely placed himself between Follansbee and the mob, which was now following the speeding soldiers. The mayor, who had nothing more than a rolled up umbrella as defense against the mob, was unsuccessfully calling for them to remain calm. He introduced himself to Captain Follansbee as Baltimore's mayor and asked him to stop running at double time, as it showed that the soldiers were in a state of panic and would further incite their pursuers. Follansbee slowed the pace. Then he said, "We are attacked without provocation," to which Brown replied, "You must defend yourselves." By marching along with the soldiers, Brown was risking his own life.

Sensing trouble, shopkeepers along Pratt Street had already shuttered their stores, as did others on nearby business streets after learning that crowds would be harassing the soldiers—more proof that the city was aware that trouble would arise from the presence of Union soldiers. Brown says it was the city's merchants who found the cartload of sand and were responsible for placing it across the tracks. Pratt Street was now a wild scene of chaos and confusion. Shop windows and doors were broken. Shards of glass lined the streets. Businesses were sacked of any rifles, knives and pistols that might have been about. The wounded were lying on the pavement, and those who could crawled into doorways bleeding, while others sought shelter in shops or the sides of buildings. Some soldiers who slumped in doorways were helped by sympathetic citizens who tended to their wounds and led them away from the mob to safety.

The April 20 edition of the *Baltimore Sun* offered its readers the following graphic description of the chaotic scene:

As one of the soldiers fired, he was struck with a stone and knocked down, and as he attempted to arise another stone struck him in the face, when he crawled into a store and prostrating himself on the floor, clasped his hands and begged piteously for his life.

Police Chief Kane also arrived from Camden Station with a squad of about fifty police officers, all armed with pistols. They were called out to assist with crowd control. Later they would make arrests. (Busy municipal courts merely issued fines for violating ordinances against throwing missiles on the city's streets.) Once the police positioned themselves to the rear of the troops, they were able to protect their flank with drawn pistols. Telegraph poles and other obstructions were now being torn from their anchors and rolled across the rails, and the police were kept busy removing them. As quickly as they removed one pole another would be rolled in place farther down the line.

Charles Ridley's Baltimore County Horse Guards were called out to help. During the evening, they would join forces with others to destroy some of Baltimore's transportation infrastructure. One among them was Corporal Harry Gilmor who would become a major of the Confederate cavalry and would repeat his destructive performance three years later in a failed attempt by the Confederate army to once again seize Baltimore and Washington.

Farther west on Pratt Street, soldiers under Major Watson's command finally made it to Camden Station after exchanging fire with the mob. However, when they reached Howard Street, they had to leave their car and then quick-march the final two blocks, as rioters had torn up the street rails. At Camden Station, Watson's soldiers met up with Colonel Jones and were safely loaded on to a train bound for Washington. They sat and waited for Follansbee and his men. Outside the station, another mob was shouting and cursing. They were also waiting for Follansbee and his soldiers.

Before they could get to Camden Station, Follansbee and his four companies had to pass Pratt and Light Streets, where the mob was now at its fiercest and most violent. Four soldiers were either shot, stoned or beaten to death here. One of the men uttered, "All hail to the Stars and Stripes!" as he died. These were the first Union soldiers to die in battle in the Civil War. Follansbee ordered his men to go into double time again as they ran full speed along the several remaining blocks to their destination. On the way, the soldiers dragged their muskets, reloading as they sped on firing wildly on the run.

When Follansbee and his men finally showed up at Camden Station, they were pursued by one raging mob and greeted by another. Soldiers inside the waiting cars had to provide covering fire for their comrades. Once the last group was safely inside the cars, Colonel Jones ordered the soldiers to lower the blinds on the car windows to try calming the crowd.

Although no longer under attack, a nervous soldier fired from the train and killed Robert W. Davis, a well-known Baltimore businessman who was among the crowd. It was a bitter departure for those volunteers who chugged out of Camden Station, bound for Washington at about 1:30 p.m. The soldiers had left their dead and wounded comrades behind, as well as the musicians of the brigade band who also had to deal with angry crowds.

Colonel Jones, in his written report of the riot, said that an investigation revealed that Davis had thrown a brick at the railway car. Jones admitted it was not a reason to kill a man. But in explanation, he noted that his "men were infuriated beyond control" as a result of the attacks upon them and their comrades. Even though the blinds were drawn, the mob continued throwing bricks at the train. Jones had to keep his men from firing at the crowd as the train left the station for Washington. He further reported that after everyone was aboard the railroad cars at Camden Station, he took a count and found about 130 of his men were missing.

In George Brown's memoirs, written twenty-six years after these events, he tends to downplay the riot and argues that later reports made the events sound worse than the reality. He says, "The mob which was not very large, as it seemed to me, was pursuing with shouts and stones and I think an occasional pistol-shot." If that were true, the soldiers shouldn't have been firing steadily into the crowd. They had been ordered to fire only when fired upon and then only at the man firing. For the most part, the soldiers showed discipline. Watson's men did not fire while in their rail car until one of the men called out that he was wounded. And then they fired upon Watson's command to do so.

Brown portrays Robert W. Davis as a bystander, which he may very well have been. Throughout these events, after having first left a calmer Camden Station, Brown was then confined to one area alongside Captain Follansbee and Police Chief Kane. He could not see what was happening to all the soldiers who were strung out along Pratt Street. And he couldn't have seen Major Watson and his soldiers, who were past the Jones Falls Bridge, farther west along Pratt Street, on their way to Camden Station. They were also fighting off a mob that Brown could not have seen. There had to have been much confusion that day. Some observers say there were five thousand rioters along Pratt Street, belying Brown's observation that the mob was not very large.

The *Baltimore Sun*'s account of the riot states that there were men on horseback racing between Camden and President Street Stations, advising the crowds of the latest events on each end. In Brown's memoirs, he does not tell us that he was aware of any riders. So he would probably not have known what was going on elsewhere. And even from where Brown was located after he came to Follansbee's aid, marching with the soldiers and appealing to the crowd to be calm, he says he saw Chief Kane draw his pistol, face the crowd and then shout, "Keep back men, or I shoot!" Kane's desperate order was proof enough that this was becoming a very dangerous and critical situation.

The rioters were finally dispersed after the soldiers left Camden Station for Washington. At about four o'clock that afternoon, a large group of citizens gathered somewhat less aggressively, assembling in front of the courthouse at Monument Square, one of the city's important meeting places. Mayor Brown addressed them. Earlier in the day, with the assistance of Captain Follansbee and police chief George Kane, Brown tried unsuccessfully to disperse an angry mob. Now he told more sedate Baltimoreans that he was a proud citizen of Maryland and of the United States and would defend the Union but did not wish to help to war against a sister state.

Further highlighting the differences between Baltimore's politically divided citizenry was Governor Thomas H. Hicks, a Union supporter who happened to be in the city that day, traveling from the state capital at Annapolis on personal business. Hicks was a weak governor who often failed to take proper charge of situations requiring his leadership, even shifting political positions as needed. He belonged to the national Native American political party, also called the Know-Nothings. The name stuck because when asked about their political agenda, Know-Nothing members would answer that they "knew nothing." What they really did believe was that only Protestants could be elected to public office. In addition, the Know-Nothings were anti-immigrant, anti-liquor and anti-Catholic. In front of this somewhat calmer crowd, Hicks also delivered a speech expressing the same sentiments as Mayor Brown but with greater emotion.

On this evening, Hicks had reason to believe that his life was in danger, as feelings were high against him. The crowd, made up mostly of Southern sympathizers, reacted in anger when he told them that "the Union was to be preserved." Then he qualified his statement, roaring above the crowd, "I am a Marylander, and I love my State, and I love the Union, but I will suffer my right arm to be torn from my body before I will raise it to strike a sister state."

Two prominent citizens, William F. Preston and S. Teackle Wallis, also spoke. Wallis was legal counsel to a pro-Southern group. He was not a secessionist, however; he wrote editorial columns for Frank Key Howard's pro-South *Baltimore Exchange*. Others spoke before the assembly, expressing their love of the Constitution and the Union. It was clear, however, that this was becoming a gathering of Southern sympathizers led by fire-eating orators who told their audience that their hearts were with their Southern brothers and sisters.

William Preston said, "I would prefer to die defending the Constitution as maintained by the South, than live a single hour under the fanatical tyranny of the North." He was met with approving cheers. It was an emotional gathering.

Police chief George Kane, an open secessionist, sensing how the political situation was going, once again acted on his own to help heat up the situation. He sent an inflammatory wire to Bradley T. Johnson, captain of the Frederick Guards, a prominent secessionist and a future general of the Confederate cavalry. Johnson may have been pro-South, but his hometown city of Frederick was definitely pro-Union. Kane's message read:

> *Streets red with Maryland blood; send expresses over the mountains of Maryland and Virginia for the riflemen to come without delay. Fresh hordes will come down on us tomorrow. We will fight them and whip them or die.*

Shaken by the riots, Mayor Brown, Governor Hicks and John Garrett, president of the B&O Railroad, all wrote urgent letters to President Lincoln, informing him of their concerns. Garrett was a wealthy and openly Northern sympathizer who came from a slave-owning, pro-Southern family. During the Civil War, his B&O Railroad was at the service of the Union army and was, as a result, repeatedly wrecked by the South's destructive raids. Brown and Garrett were as one in trying to end any future bloodshed on Baltimore's streets. Each man wrote to Lincoln informing him that Union soldiers would no longer be permitted transit through Baltimore or be allowed to use the railroad, as it would encourage riots and imperil citizens, as well as the soldiers. Brown was concerned for his city; Garrett was concerned for his rails and rolling stock.

"The city," wrote Brown, "was facing a vociferous army of howling wolves." Governor Hicks added in his own letter that "it is not possible for many soldiers to pass through Baltimore unless they fight their way at every step."

The first deadly battle of the Civil War had been fought on Baltimore's streets, and President Abraham Lincoln declined to immediately respond to any letters telling him to stop the movement of troops to Washington.

CHAPTER VI

More Violence

Baltimore Is Cut Off from the North, April 19–27, 1861

The bodies of the Massachusetts soldiers could not be sent out to Boston as you requested, all communication between this city and Philadelphia by railroad and with Boston by steamer have ceased.
—*Telegram from Mayor George Brown to Massachusetts governor John A. Andrew, April 20, 1861*

After the meeting at Monument Square, night fell on a divided city with groups of men and women gathering at street corners throughout Baltimore to discuss the terrible events of the day. Gangs were now roaming the city armed with knives, pistols and rifles, many of which had been looted from shops. About 9:00 p.m., the tempers of some of the citizens were still boiling, and a ragtag group returned to the President Street Station, where they broke down a door and smashed in waiting room windows. A demand was made of railroad employees to turn over such muskets and rifles as were available in the station. One of the employees explained there were none in the building. After appointing a committee to search the depot and satisfying themselves there were no arms there, the mob left.

Southern sympathizers from Baltimore's surrounding areas were now traveling the roads to the city like Revolutionary War minutemen. "The Lexington of 1861," the gathering was called. They were prepared to assist fellow secessionists to deliver the city and state into the Southern camp.

Also at nine o'clock that evening, another large crowd gathered in front of Barnum's Hotel on the other side of Monument Square. Barnum's was one of the city's finest hotels and a well-known meeting place for Southern

Barnum's Hotel, a favorite meeting place on Monument Square. *Courtesy Enoch Pratt Free Library, Maryland's State Resource Center, Baltimore, MD.*

sympathizers. Here, from a balcony, ex-governor and open secessionist Enoch L. Lowe excited his audience by telling them that "Frederick County would lend assistance to Baltimore to the extent of their power."

Members of Charles Ridgley's Baltimore County Cavalry, their duty under an assignment to contain the riot now fulfilled, turned to manufacturing some spectacular mayhem of their own. Corporal Harry Gilmor, Lieutenant John Merryman and others joined together from outlying counties and cities. They were led by police chief George Kane and Isaac Ridgeway Trimble, acting under orders from Mayor Brown, Governor Hicks, Chief Kane and Enoch Lowe. The four men met in Hicks's hotel room, where the governor was now confined after his speech, as he was so ill he could not stand. After receiving their orders, Kane and Trimble began systematically destroying bridges, rails and telegraph lines leading into the city from the north. The intent was to prevent further movement of troops from the North into Baltimore, avoiding further riots.

Isaac Ridgeway Trimble was a West Point graduate who, after resigning from the army, went into railroading. Trimble, who was called "Colonel," became one of America's outstanding railroad construction executives. He built many railroad systems in Maryland and the nearby Mid-Atlantic states. It was Trimble who built the President Street Station in 1849–50. At the time, it was America's largest railroad depot. Armed with Trimble's unique railroad knowledge, the men began tearing up railroad tracks efficiently and

One of the bridges spanning the region's many rivers later destroyed by Southern sympathizers. *Courtesy Enoch Pratt Free Library, Maryland's State Resource Center, Baltimore, MD.*

with precision, destroying and burning the bridges used by the Philadelphia Railroad Line, which ran over the Bush and Gunpowder Rivers a few miles north of Baltimore. Maryland's Purnell Legion destroyed three bridges belonging to the PW&B and then three more belonging to the Northern Central Railroad. All these bridges ran from the north into the city. They also blockaded major roads and cut telegraph lines leading into Baltimore from the north. A later observer noted how efficient the destruction had been. Trimble had instructed his men well. Although Brown, Kane and Lowe said that they ordered the destruction in an effort to keep Union soldiers out of Baltimore and to avoid further riots, Governor Hicks, as could be expected, later denied issuing such an order.

From every part of Maryland, men rushed to join their Baltimore brothers, until the city looked like a Southern stronghold. Shouts of praise for the South were heard everywhere, and Mayor Brown observed that on that day, for the first time, men were singing "Dixie." When dawn rose on Saturday morning, April 20, Baltimore was reeling. If something wasn't done and done immediately, the cities of Washington and Baltimore might possibly fall to the South. There was no doubt that a second and more dangerous riot would break out at the least excitement.

By April 21, Lincoln, who had not immediately answered the messages from Brown, Hicks and Garrett, was now aware from reports that Baltimore's riot was not merely a local situation but a significant national event that he could not permit to accelerate. He was facing a real crisis. There were already dispatches from the South that at Norfolk, Virginia, Southerners were commandeering vessels belonging to Northern owners. And there were more reports detailing great jubilation in Baltimore over Virginia's recent secession announcement. Lincoln had to act swiftly and decisively. Troops would have to pass safely through Baltimore to defend the capital city, with or without Baltimore's permission, or Lincoln would have to do the unthinkable: abandon the city of Washington to the Confederates. Trying to resolve this dilemma, Lincoln invited Governor Hicks and Mayor Brown to meet with him and sent on the following message:

> *I desire to consult with you and the Mayor of Baltimore to preserve the peace of Maryland. Please come immediately by special train which you can take at Baltimore or if necessary one can be sent from here. Answer forthwith.*
> A. Lincoln

Hicks could not attend, giving a lame and insufficient excuse for his absence. After advising Washington that the governor was unavailable, Brown was asked to come anyway. He arrived with three prominent Baltimoreans, one of whom was the lawyer S. Teackle Wallis, who would later share imprisonment in Boston Harbor's Fort Warren with Brown. They met at Lincoln's home in the White House, and it was, according to Brown's account, at the outset at least, a cordial visit. Toward the end of the meeting, however, Brown and his group were dealt a stern ultimatum. Lincoln—in the presence of Winfield Scott, commanding general of the Union army, and cabinet members, including Simon Cameron, secretary of war—opened the conference. He made it clear that there was no intention on the part of the Union to wage war on the South. The call for volunteers, Lincoln explained, was for the defense of Washington and to protect Federal property throughout the Union. His proclamation was misunderstood by the public, Lincoln claimed, adding, "I am not a learned man, I am not a learned man." The president and Scott advised Brown that they would earnestly try to avoid moving troops through Baltimore. They proposed using the Chesapeake Bay and Annapolis as alternate routes to bring in the soldiers by sea and a land route through the Annapolis-based rail lines.

Lincoln already knew that Governor Hicks, although an outspoken Union supporter, was nevertheless weak in his dealings with the secessionist groups in his legislature. They would never endorse the option of allowing troops to move through Annapolis or the Bay. At present, neither option could realistically be accomplished until Union troops controlled the region and repaired the damaged rails and bridges around Annapolis. Brown wanted assurances that no troops would come through Baltimore again. Lincoln then told his visitors, "If I grant you this concession and no troops shall move through the city [Baltimore], you will be back here tomorrow demanding that none shall be marched around it." Lincoln said it half joking and with a smile.

Lincoln and Scott emphasized that if traveling through Annapolis was not possible, they could not make any definite promises to Brown about not using the city in the future as a transit point through to Washington. Baltimore would be avoided only if there was a guarantee that the alternate routes would remain open and safe for troop movements. It sounded as if Lincoln and Scott were being conciliatory. However, that was not the case. Brown was asked to ensure that Baltimoreans would not interfere with troops outside the city. Brown thought for a while and replied that he would do his best but could not guarantee what happened out of his legal and political

Annapolis. At right is the U.S. Naval Academy. The sailing vessel may be the *Constitution*. The domed building at center is the state capitol. *Courtesy Enoch Pratt Free Library, Maryland's State Resource Center, Baltimore, MD.*

jurisdiction of Baltimore. Obviously, the only one who could help with that request was the absent and unreliable Governor Hicks.

With Brown's unsatisfactory answer, Scott warned him and his colleagues that if Union soldiers could not get to Washington by any alternate routes, "they would have to fight their way through Baltimore." Unbeknownst to Brown, General Scott and Lincoln had already decided that they would be prepared to bombard Baltimore and other Maryland cities into submission in order to safely move Union troops. Clearly, Baltimore was now a victim of its strategic location.

Within the week, Lincoln would finally lose his patience and issue his radical order, General Order 100, of April 27, 1861. This order imposed martial law and suspended habeas corpus in Baltimore and parts of Maryland, covering Annapolis, to ensure protection for the Union and his capital city. With the suspension of civil law and habeas corpus, Lincoln had set in motion a constitutional crisis, one of the earliest in American history. Soldiers could now arrest and imprison citizens without formal charges and for an undetermined period of time.

Destruction of the northern approaches to Baltimore had been executed effectively and with precision, thanks to Isaac Trimble's expert knowledge. That news was brought home with a series of telegraph messages passing between Colonel Jones, Chief Kane, Mayor Brown and John A. Andrew, the governor of Massachusetts. Jones requested of Kane that the bodies of the four dead New Englanders be sent to Boston. Brown informed Governor Andrew that the bodies could not be returned immediately, as all transportation to the North had been cut off, including steamship service to Boston. Brown assured Governor Andrew that the bodies would be well cared for in sealed cement caskets until proper transportation was resumed. He added that the city would bear all the necessary expenses. The Baltimore City Council had already set aside money for recompense for the dead and wounded soldiers to be delivered to Governor Andrew and doled out as he saw fit.

Governor Andrew wired back, thanking Brown for his attention and courtesy. Then Andrew added an acerbic sentiment that might have been on the minds of many Northerners that day:

> *I am overwhelmed with surprise that a peaceful march of American citizens over the highway to the defense of our common capital should be deemed aggressive to Baltimoreans. Through New York the march was triumphal.*

It would take a while before any troops or even peaceful civilians could get to Baltimore by rail. On April 28, ten days after the riot, J. Edgar Thomson, president of the Pennsylvania Central Railroad, wrote to Simon Cameron, secretary of war, emphasizing the almost complete destruction of his road. He went on to advise Cameron that if there were any citizens of Baltimore loyal to the Union, they were definitely in a minority. Then he added that the City of Baltimore should be made to pay for the restoration that would have to be effected to put his damaged systems back in operation.

CHAPTER VII

Lincoln Declares Martial Law

April 27 to May 13, 1861

*If it become[s] necessary then resort to the bombardment of their cities—and of course
the suspension of the writ of habeas corpus.*
—*Abraham Lincoln's order to General Winfield Scott*

Baltimore was now a city in chaos and under arms. It was a dangerous
and ominous situation full of peril for the nation's lightly defended
capital, less than forty miles to the south. In Baltimore, Isaac Trimble now
headed an army of fifteen thousand men patched together with the help
of the city's police. While this group was ready to defend the city, not all its
defenders were armed.

Three days after the Pratt Street Riot, twenty-six hundred more
Pennsylvania volunteers, bound to defend Washington, were able to cross
the border between these two states. They came by train into Maryland but
could get only as far as Ashland, near Cockeysville, just north of Baltimore.
Their train could proceed no further because of the earlier destruction of
the rails. Wildly excited, two horsemen dashed into Baltimore notifying the
citizenry of the intrusion, shouting, "The Yankees are coming!"

Notice of the soldiers' arrival was also received in Washington on April
22, via telegram sent by John Garrett of the B&O to George Brown while
he was meeting with Lincoln. The telegram informed Brown that there
were gatherings of armed Marylanders prepared to attack the soldiers, and
another riot was possible. Brown received the telegram just after he and his
colleagues left their meeting with the president. Brown returned to the White
House to tell Lincoln of these new and disturbing events. Lincoln assured

him that he had no knowledge of this movement and had not ordered it. It was agreed that the Pennsylvanians would be sent back to their homes.

Meanwhile, at Ashland the soldiers had already been met by an opposing force of civilians, who were armed and ready to make a fight. The Pennsylvanians, who thought they were going straight on to Washington in a matter of a few hours, had brought little food with them. Some had only crackers. Most lacked arms, expecting to receive weapons upon arrival in Washington. The soldiers finally encamped in the area, settled down and waited for further instructions. Senator Anthony Kennedy and Congressman J.M. Harris, both from Maryland, stepped in between the two groups to resolve a potential and unwanted clash.

At this early stage of the Civil War, it was obvious that neither the South nor the North was as yet anxious to go to battle. Cool heads were trying very hard to prevent the attack on Fort Sumter and the riot in Baltimore from getting out of control and exploding into a full-scale conflict. Even the hotheaded pro-Southern Baltimore police chief, George Kane, arranged for the Pennsylvanians to be fed and receive some badly needed medical treatment. Some of the soldiers had fallen ill while they were waiting at their encampment, and two even died.

The Pennsylvanians finally returned home. But in Baltimore, the population was still filled with memories of the excitement of the riot and harangues, and there were calls by prominent citizens to take the road to secession. The city was now awash with Confederate flags flying everywhere, while only a few Union flags could be seen.

One place where the American flag was still prominent was high above the ramparts of Fort McHenry. It was rumored around town that the fort was scheduled to be attacked. The mob finally acted when it approached Captain John Robinson, commandant of Fort McHenry. This group of Baltimoreans was led by one of the police commissioners, John W. Davis. Davis advised Robinson that they had come to protect the fort. Robinson thought otherwise; they were there to take over the fort. He told them he knew they were there to attack and take control of a Federal facility. Robinson had already been hearing some strong pro-Southern speeches just outside Fort McHenry. And only the Maryland flag was flown at those meetings. Robinson advised Commissioner Davis that if his men came past a certain line that he pointed out to them, located outside the fort, he would open fire. When asked if he would dare fire into the city and harm women and children, Robinson said, "Yes," although he would not be pleased to do so. Finally, Robinson added, "I assure you…if your Baltimore mob comes down here tonight, you will not have another mob in Baltimore for ten years to come, sir." With this, Commissioner Davis left, never to return.

The situation was tense. In an attempt to defuse a new riot, the Baltimore City Council forbade the flying of any flags, except those of the United States set above Federal buildings. Vital buoy markers necessary for safe navigation in the Basin and in and out of Baltimore Harbor had been removed, making vessel movements dangerous at the least. Stores were shut. Merchants were complaining that they were unable to carry on with business. Armed gangs were still roaming the streets. According to observers who later described the growing crisis, had the mobs taken the decision to act with force, Maryland might well have seceded from the Union. Abraham Lincoln was looking at Baltimore and thinking of ways to prevent a situation rapidly moving out of control.

On April 22, another group of Baltimoreans, this time made up of private citizens and businessmen, also made demands of Lincoln that he not allow any troops to travel through their city. They went a step further; they wanted Lincoln to make peace with the CSA, honorably or otherwise. Lincoln got angry. He was remembered as saying:

> *There is no Washington in that, no Jackson in that, no manhood and no honor in that...Go home and tell your people that if they will not attack us, we will not attack them; but if they do attack us, we will return it and that severely.*

Lincoln was probably thinking about the decision he, Scott and his cabinet had already made to bomb into submission any opposition within the state. It was meetings such as these that made Lincoln realize he could not allow the situation to continue. Washington had to be defended. He would have to act.

This volatile situation was saved by a portly, forty-three-year-old, politically oriented lawyer with a brusque personality who was also a brigadier general of the Massachusetts Militia. He was Benjamin Franklin Butler, a Democrat, a state legislator, a future congressman and a future governor of Massachusetts. Butler was a backer of Vice President John Breckinridge, one of Lincoln's three rivals in the 1860 presidential election. Butler was not thinking of politics when he quickly took control of his Eighth Massachusetts Militia with determination, a tough approach and stunning speed. Leading his men to Washington was his mission; that he would succeed at that task, Butler had no doubt. He was also prone to making swift decisions and brash, unthinking statements that he would afterward regret. "When we come from Massachusetts," he announced with some braggadocio, "we will not leave a single traitor behind, unless he is hanging upon a tree." As far as Butler was concerned, Maryland was hostile territory.

This crusty soldier imagined that there would be a slave revolt in Maryland. Then he topped off that startling idea by advising Marylanders that he could put an armed soldier in any house in Maryland whenever he had a mind to. With respect to his slave riot threat, Butler later wrote a letter to Governor Hicks, assuring him that he was ever ready to prevent any civil disorders occasioned by slaves. Once, when he believed one of his soldiers had been poisoned by a Marylander, he threatened to put poison in the homes of suspected persons. After a medical examination, it was determined that the soldier had died of cholera.

On April 20, Butler, charged with controlling the area in and around Baltimore and Annapolis and getting the damaged rails running, bypassed Baltimore after learning of the destruction of the approaches to the city. First, he led his troops as far as he could by train, to a point north of Baltimore where the Susquehanna River empties into the Chesapeake Bay. There he commandeered the railroad ferry *Maryland*, loaded his troops aboard and sailed on to Annapolis, occupying that city on the twenty-first. Butler also took control of the United States Naval Academy. Then he ordered his men to repair the tracks of the Annapolis and Elk Ridge Railway, which had been earlier ripped up by marauding bands of secessionists. Armed troops boarded specially constructed flatcars armed with Howitzers to keep gangs from doing further damage along the lines.

While Butler occupied Annapolis, Governor Hicks finally gave in to pressure from pro-Southern politicians calling for a special legislative session to determine whether Maryland should secede from the Union. Butler's presence in the capital city forced Hicks to move the legislature to the pro-Union city of Frederick.

On April 24, Virginia made a formal invitation, carried to Frederick personally by James Mason, an ex U.S. senator, urging Maryland's legislators to join with Virginia in a mutual defense pact. The Maryland legislature declined the offer, and its senate claimed that it did not have the power to consider the issue. It then voted to close down the session over the howls and noisy protests of the secessionist bloc.

In order to get Union troops to Washington as swiftly as possible and with the least opposition, Lincoln agreed to route troops through the Chesapeake Bay or via rail on the newly repaired tracks around Annapolis. Butler's

Annapolis Junction. After repairing this facility, Butler used it to avoid Baltimore and send troops to Washington. *Courtesy Enoch Pratt Free Library, Maryland's State Resource Center, Baltimore, MD.*

tight grip over the Annapolis area was vital in order to allow this free and uneventful movement of troops. Now, Butler, without receiving any formal order or permission to do so, took command of New York's recently arrived Seventh Regiment. He quickly sent these men on to Washington by way of a long march over a hastily reconstructed bridge through to Annapolis Junction, where they boarded a special train waiting to take them on to the capital. The New Yorkers arrived on April 24, to Lincoln's great relief. They were the first soldiers to reach the capital since the Massachusetts militiamen who were able to leave Baltimore on the same day of the Pratt Street Riot.

Before the arrival of the New Yorkers, Lincoln was in a desperate mood. He has been said to have asked, "What's holding them up, why don't they come?" Well aware that only the Potomac River separated the South from his capital, Lincoln waited fruitlessly and in fear of a Southern attack for more than a week. This was the effect of Baltimore's Pratt Street Riot on the fate of the nation's capital. The Union was still unable to send on enough troops to properly defend Washington.

Daily, Lincoln would be informed that his high-ranking soldiers and sailors were leaving the city to join up with the Confederacy. Among those resigning to serve with the South was one of the country's most talented officers, Robert E. Lee. Even Winfield Scott, his superior officer, could not convince him to stay with the North. Should the South attack Washington, not only was the city indefensible, but there were also many secessionists living there who would doubtless rise up to help an invading Confederate army.

Before the arrival of New York's Seventh Regiment, Lincoln visited the ward where the wounded soldiers of the Pratt Street Riot lay in their beds. He was in a dark mood that day. As he paced among them, he kept saying that there were no reinforcements and no North. "You are the only Northern reality," he said sadly.

That Washington was not invaded was further proof that neither side was anxious to engage in an all-out war at this stage of the rebellion. Lincoln finally accepted the reality that Baltimore needed to be pacified and opened up to allow a safe and ready corridor between the city and Washington. Finally, on April 27, he was to take drastic measures and order martial law. His Executive Order 100 read:

> *Executive order*
> *To the Commanding General of the Army of the United States:*
> *You are engaged in repressing an insurrection against the laws of the United States. If at any point on or in the vicinity of the military line used between the city of Philadelphia, via Perryville* [Maryland, Annapolis City] *and Annapolis Junction you find resistance it is necessary to suspend habeas corpus for the public safety, you personally or through the officer in command at the point where the resistance occurs are authorized to suspend the writ.*
> *A. Lincoln*

Meanwhile, Butler had been sweeping through the Annapolis area pacifying the region and repairing bridges and rail tracks, slowly restoring transportation into Baltimore and ensuring a secure transit south through the Chesapeake Bay so that he could send more troops to Washington. He restored the B&O's rail system to working order while increasing security over the area around Annapolis. Then, extending the B&O's range outward, Butler, under orders from General Winfield Scott, had his men finally open up the line's station into Baltimore at Relay, just seven miles outside the city's limits.

At Annapolis, he ordered his soldiers to protect the sailing ship USS *Constitution*, docked at the U.S. Naval Academy, and then crewed it with those of his men with seafaring experience. On April 24, the government ordered the naval academy closed and sent the USS *Constitution* sailing to the north, with the academy's midshipmen who had not defected to the South, to Newport, Rhode Island, where they continued with their military training.

Events were developing so fast that officials in Washington were cut off from many of the fields of action. The government lacked real knowledge and information about what was happening. Butler remained cool, often acting on his own without any orders from his superiors. There is no doubt that his decisive actions put Maryland, and especially Baltimore, under tight control, frustrating the ambitions of Maryland's secessionists.

On May 11, Butler claimed to have information that one thousand men made up of Baltimore gangs, all of whom were sworn to kill a soldier, planned to attack him at Annapolis. Another group coming from a different direction was also alleged to have been involved in the supposed attack. Butler advised Mayor Brown to keep his Baltimore toughs from leaving the city. Brown reports in his memoir that it was all a fiction, and no attack was ever planned or even occurred.

On May 13, Butler moved five hundred of his Eighth Massachusetts Militia, which included some men who were veterans of the Pratt Street Riot, together with a battery of six cannons manned by the Bostonians of Major Cook's Artillery, into Baltimore. They came from Relay by train to

A view of Federal Hill before 1861. *Courtesy Enoch Pratt Free Library, Maryland's State Resource Center, Baltimore MD.*

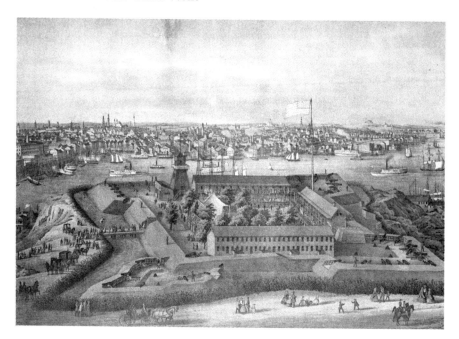

Federal Hill and its fortification as they appeared after the riot. *Courtesy Enoch Pratt Free Library, Maryland's State Resource Center, Baltimore, MD.*

the now accessible Camden Station. Night was falling on the city, and the soldiers slogged through a heavy rainstorm accompanied by thunder and lightning. Covered by the growing darkness and foul weather, Butler's men marched silently, while Cook's Bostonians hauled their six cannons up to the strategic heights at Federal Hill, where they all worked throughout the night digging in and setting up defenses and ordinance, while hastily creating a strategic military camp.

Butler had trumped the city overnight. When Baltimoreans awoke the next morning, they were looking into the mouths of six menacing cannons, one of which was aimed directly at Monument Square, the political and social heart of their city. The square was home to the Battle Monument, the statue of Lady Baltimore commemorating the city's defeat of the British during the War of 1812. Barnum's Hotel and Gilmor House, two of Baltimore's finest hotels, faced the square, as did the Masonic House, which housed the Federal court. Some of the finest homes belonging to the city's wealthiest citizens were also located here. Later, General Dix, at the time military governor of Baltimore, told some visitors to the fort on Federal Hill that one of his cannons was always aimed at Monument Square. At the first

The Gilmor Hotel, located at Monument Square. *Courtesy Enoch Pratt Free Library, Maryland's State Resource Center, Baltimore, MD.*

This is what Baltimoreans awoke to after Butler entered Baltimore by night on May 13. *Courtesy Enoch Pratt Free Library, Maryland's State Resource Center, Baltimore, MD.*

sign of trouble, he could see the monument and destroy the square with one shot of his cannon.

The American flag now flew boldly above the military encampment for the whole city to see. Butler notified the citizens of Baltimore that they were under military occupation and from now on would be forbidden to do anything against the security interests of the Union. With this deft maneuver, Butler took a long step toward ensuring that there would be no more riots in Baltimore and that Union troops could now move safely through the city. From now on, Baltimore would have to behave. Butler's move reduced tensions in the city and kept Southern agitators from becoming bolder in trying to push Maryland into the Confederacy.

General Winfield Scott, commanding general of the Union army, and President Lincoln were not impressed with Butler's latest tactic. Lincoln was concerned, but Scott was furious and relieved that the occupation of the city had been accomplished without creating another riot and "without force of arms." But too often Butler acted without authority from his superiors or worse, without even advising them of his plans. Aside from its military effect, Butler's Baltimore move could have created many unpleasant political consequences. Scott promptly relieved Butler of his command, turning it over to General George Cadwalader, who made Fort McHenry his home base.

Butler had held his command for less than a month. In that time, he funneled enough troops into Washington to help defend the capital. He repaired the destroyed rail lines and bridges running to Baltimore and controlled the Annapolis area with a strong hand, allowing him to have unrestricted use of the Chesapeake Bay and permitting free movement to Washington and Baltimore via the bay and by rail. Butler cut off most of the heavy flow of military supplies that had been freely shipped to the South through Maryland. Butler also captured large caches of illegal equipment and arms, which he sent on to Fort McHenry, and he opened up the city of Baltimore through military control.

Despite the crackdown, Butler was still unable to prevent hundreds of men from crossing the Potomac to join the forces of the CSA. Harry Gilmor relates in his book, *Four Years in the Saddle*, that in the month of August, three months after Butler had taken over the city, he was able to easily cross the lightly patrolled Potomac River to meet up with some of his friends of the Baltimore County Horse Guards in Virginia. Butler had calmed the troublesome city of Baltimore and defused a critical situation that, had it not been handled properly, could have ended with the embarrassment of having the nation's capital winding up in Southern hands.

Because of his outstanding but heavy-handed performance, Butler could blame no one but himself for his dismissal. He created enemies among the citizenry and often acted without orders. One year later, Butler's difficult reputation would follow him to New Orleans. Lincoln, who understood that Butler knew how to pacify a population, promoted him to major general and appointed him military governor of that city. In New Orleans, his tough and arbitrary administration earned him the nasty nickname "Beast Butler."

The 1860s lacked electronic communication, yet somehow bad news traveled fast in America. Telegraphs, railroads, newspapers and magazines carried the story of the riot. The speed with which the events on Baltimore's Pratt Street reached the rest of the country was one of the reasons Americans were emotionally agitated. Rallies for and against the riot were held in cities throughout the country.

In New York City, for example, six days after the riot a military group met and cried out, "Go through Baltimore or die!" The *New York Herald* proposed that Union troops should "cut their way to Baltimore." However, New York's mayor, Fernando Wood, had already advocated that the city sever itself from the Union and carry on as a separate city-state. Americans recognized that unlike at Fort Sumter, in Baltimore men had died by shots fired in the anger and rage fomented by an unruly mob. At Fort Sumter, polite and civil notes had been exchanged between the opponents, and friendly negotiations were held before any shots or hostilities began. And there were no deaths there. Even after Union forces surrendered the fort, General P.G.T. Beauregard graciously permitted the defeated Union forces to withdraw with the gentlemanly permission to fire a salute to the American flag.

Baltimore was different. There had been a full-blown and nasty riot with taunts and rocks and other missiles flying. Then there were the bullets. Perhaps the Sixth Massachusetts might have acted a bit too hastily. Nevertheless, from all reports, the soldiers did not fire the first shots. But then there was the man called Davis. He was a popular and well-respected citizen who, it was claimed, was not menacing the soldiers. He was cut down by a shot fired from a secure train at Camden Station after the riot had abated. That news was not well received in the city and undoubtedly increased the level of anger. Despite some real efforts to defuse the crisis, high passion was still running in the city. Baltimore was resounding with calls to keep out further troop movements and also secede from the Union.

Soon after the Pratt Street Riot, a native Marylander, James Ryder Randall, living in Louisiana and teaching at a college near New Orleans, read of the death of a friend in a newspaper report (actually, his friend survived a severe injury). Filled with grief and angered by the North's attempts to prevent secession from the Union, Randall wrote a poem, "My Maryland." It was composed and published within one short week after the Pratt Street Riot, appearing in the *New Orleans Delta* on April 26. Filled with allusions to the state's history, the South's greatness and the perfidiousness of the North, Randall wrote specifically of the Pratt Street Riot:

> *Avenge the patriotic gore*
> *that flecked the streets of Baltimore*
> *and be the battle queen of yore*
> *Maryland my Maryland!*

The unhappy Randall also attacked Lincoln, calling him a despot, a tyrant and, in one stanza, a vandal:

> *Thou will not yield the vandal toll*
> *Maryland!*
> *Thou will not crook to his control*
> *Maryland!*

Union general Benjamin F. Butler.
Courtesy Library of Congress.

"Maryland, My Maryland" song sheet.
Courtesy Library of Congress.

Randall's nine-stanza poem was an immediate sensation in the South and, of course, in Maryland. Appealing to Southerners with its attacks on Lincoln and the North and references to the South's glory, two sisters, Jennie and Hettie Cary, residents of Baltimore, quickly prepared an edited version of the poem (changing the poem's title to "Maryland, My Maryland"), which was then set to the German melody "O Tannenbaum." Throughout the Civil War, Confederate soldiers adopted "Maryland, My Maryland" as one of their regular battle songs. In 1939, the Maryland legislature enshrined the work as the state's anthem, memorializing for its citizens, and especially the citizens of Baltimore, one of the few positive results of the Pratt Street Riot.

CHAPTER VIII

Some Questionable Arrests

He has affected to render the military independent of and superior to the Civil Power...
For depriving us in many cases of the benefit of Trial by Jury.
—Some of the grievances set forth against King George by American colonists in the
Declaration of Independence

Another sad result of the Pratt Street Riot was Lincoln's decision to impose martial law in Baltimore and strategic parts of the state of Maryland. Closely allied to the ancient writ of habeas corpus, the use of martial law is also a radical step in controlling rebellious citizens. Martial law substitutes military rule and military law for that of civilian control and civil law. Habeas corpus requires that a person or government detaining someone without a specific legal complaint or charge produce or release that person, absent the filing of a formal charge against him.

Habeas corpus is a time-honored legal safeguard against a government's arbitrary action. Beginning with the arrest of police chief George Kane on April 27, pursuant to Lincoln's order of martial law of the same day, Benjamin Butler's silent entry into Baltimore on May 13 and throughout the Civil War, citizens of Maryland, and especially Baltimore, would be viewed by the military with suspicion for the rest of the war. The city was destined to live under military authority. For the men and women of Baltimore, there would be no regular access to civilian courts, nor could they count on the protection of many constitutional guarantees. It was the price they would pay for the Pratt Street Riot.

The arrest of Marshal Kane, the first arrest after Lincoln ordered martial law. *Courtesy Library of Congress.*

Soldiers in Monument Square anticipating a riot after Marshal Kane's arrest. *Courtesy Enoch Pratt Free Library, Maryland's State Resource Center, Baltimore, MD.*

Lincoln's use of martial law and the suspension of habeas corpus was determined illegal by the United States Supreme Court. As the nation's chief executive, he usurped the power of Congress, the nation's legislature. He stepped outside the boundaries of the separation of powers set forth in the Constitution. Yet, the president, as commander in chief of the armed forces, is the nation's supreme military leader. Some scholars of constitutional law argued that Lincoln, in such capacity, could have legally declared martial law on his own account and need not have applied to Congress for its consent. These scholars further point out that Congress, by remaining silent through inaction, tacitly approved the president's action. Harsh and often capricious, the installation of martial law and the suspension of habeas corpus would be one of Baltimore's bitter legacies resulting from the riot.

As late as April 26, 1865, more than two weeks after General Robert E. Lee's surrender of his Confederate forces at Appomattox, military authorities arrested Maryland congressman Benjamin Harris, charging him with aiding and comforting the enemy. His crime was giving two penniless Confederate soldiers, on their way home, a dollar each for lodgings. A military court found him guilty and sentenced him to three years in prison. The unfortunate congressman was later released by President Andrew Johnson and allowed to return to his duties in Washington.

In Baltimore, Moses Weisenfeld, a manufacturer of ready-made clothing and a well-known pro-Union advocate, was arrested when buttons used on Confederate uniforms were found in his factory. He claimed that some unhappy workers had placed them there to implicate him in a false crime. Even powerful friends like Johns Hopkins and Leopold Blumenberg, a Union army officer and a decorated veteran of the Battle of Antietam whom Lincoln later appointed to the office of provost marshal of Baltimore, were unable to keep Weisenfeld from prison. He spent two years in an Albany, New York prison after he was found guilty by a military court.

Then there was the indefensible manner of arresting and dragging Judge R.B. Carmichael from his courtroom in the town of Easton on Maryland's Eastern Shore. With 125 soldiers and deputies, the military occupied the town and surrounded the courthouse. After entering the building and taking Judge Carmichael into custody, one of the arrestors pistol-whipped him into unconsciousness. Six months after carrying him senseless from his courtroom and imprisoning him in three different facilities, the judge was finally released.

Before the Civil War, no American president had ever resorted to suspending habeas corpus. Thomas Jefferson toyed with the idea when he tried to bring Aaron Burr to justice. Even then he was prepared to refer the matter to Congress. Andrew Jackson, as the general commanding the American army at New Orleans, in 1814 declared martial law in that city. When a man arrested for criticizing Jackson applied for release through a writ of habeas corpus, Jackson went a step further than Lincoln would take fifty years later. Jackson ordered the judge who issued the writ of habeas corpus escorted out of town. After Jackson's famous defeat of the British at the Battle of New Orleans, the judge, having returned to his courtroom, fined the general $1,000 for contempt of court, a sum that Jackson paid.

Ross Winans, a well-known Baltimore inventor, industrial designer, manufacturer of locomotives and railroad equipment and a pro-South Maryland state legislator, was arrested twice and released soon after on both occasions, the last time only after he agreed to sign a parole. A technologically advanced steam cannon that Winans designed and that was said to be readied for delivery to the South was confiscated by Union soldiers.

The military made no effort to distinguish a person's political or social position in Baltimore's community. Mayor George Brown was arrested at his home in the early hours of the morning, as was Judge James Bartol of the Maryland Court of Appeals, the state's highest court. Bartol would become the court's chief judge in 1867. And the military would shut down the newspaper the *St. Mary's Beacon* and imprison its editor, J.S. Downs, for printing anti-Lincoln editorials

At 2:00 a.m. on May 25, 1861, without any legal authority or warrant, Union soldiers rousted John Merryman from his bed, arresting him in his Baltimore County home on a military order issued by a Union officer from Pennsylvania. Merryman was an officer in the cavalry unit that had burned the bridges leading to Baltimore the night of the Pratt Street Riot. After his arrest, Merryman was bundled off to Fort McHenry without any formal charges filed against him. He was told informally that he was accused of treason and rebellion. No witnesses were named, and no specific acts amounting to treason or rebellion were cited. The next day, Merryman's attorneys appeared at Baltimore's Federal district court and, after filing a petition on their client's behalf, persuaded a judge to hold a hearing with respect to his release pursuant to a writ of habeas corpus. The court's order was rejected by Fort McHenry's commanding officer, General George Cadwalader, after a Federal marshal served him with the process. Cadwalader told the marshal bearing the writ that he was acting under orders of his superior officers and could not deliver up the prisoner. The same day, Merryman's lawyers appealed to the Supreme Court of the United States.

Fort McHenry during the Civil War. It housed prisoners and the wounded. *Courtesy Enoch Pratt Free Library, Maryland's State Resource Center, Baltimore, MD.*

The Supreme Court's chief justice, Roger Taney, traveled to Baltimore on May 27 to act on Merryman's petition, as Maryland was the circuit for which he was responsible. He already knew the army would never deliver Merryman to Washington. Taney realized the importance of what he was about to do. He was sitting on a case involving a constitutional crisis. "I am an old man, a very old man, but perhaps I have been preserved for this occasion," he said after the hearing was over. Preserved he certainly was. At eighty-four, he was physically very fragile, requiring the assistance of his hand on his grandson's arm just to help him shuffle across the steps of Baltimore's United States Circuit Court House, located at the Masonic Lodge Building in Monument Square. Traveling to the city must have been a great physical effort for him. As he approached the courthouse, the crowd that had gathered in anticipation of his arrival removed their hats and stood in reverential silence to greet the former Baltimorean.

Prior to the formal hearing, Taney made some remarks after the marshal informed the justice that Merryman was not present, as his order to General Cadwalader required him to be. Cadwalader, who was also summoned, failed to appear. He explained his refusal to do so in a letter addressed to Taney and carried to court by a subordinate. He was following his superior's orders, Cadwalader wrote, adding that they were "executed [martial law] with judgment and discretion." Cadwalader went on to further advise the judge that "errors if any, should be made on the side of safety to the country."

CHIEF JUSTICE ROGER B. TANEY

Chief Justice of the United States Supreme Court Roger Taney. *Courtesy Library of Congress.*

The chief justice noted that he had the power to order the marshal to assemble a *posse comitatus* to bring both Merryman and Cadwalader to the court. Taney, however, was a realist. He knew that trying to get physical control of Merryman at Fort McHenry was useless. A marshal's posse could hardly overpower the numerically superior force at the fort. Perhaps he was reminded of another Supreme Court justice, his predecessor and also a chief justice. John Marshall had found President Andrew Jackson's open violation of Indian treaties unconstitutional. The decision caused Jackson to make his famous remark: "He has made the law, now let him enforce it." Of course, Marshall, like Taney, lacked the means to enforce his decision. Taney observed that he could arrest and fine Cadwalader for failing to appear before the court after being properly summoned. He declined to do that as well.

Justice Taney listened to the facts and then produced a reasoned decision in one of America's landmark civil rights cases, ex *parte Merryman.* He agreed with the prisoner's attorneys that Merryman should be released. He gave his reasons in a scathing opinion.

The chief justice attacked Lincoln not only for illegally assuming the power to suspend habeas corpus but also for improperly authorizing others in the military to use that power. By the terms of the Constitution, only Congress is authorized to suspend the writ of habeas corpus, Taney wrote, admonishing Lincoln. He went on to explain the history, origin and development of habeas corpus. It was, he said, an unalterable right that could not be taken away except by a carefully considered legislative act. The chief justice further scolded Lincoln, reminding him that under our Constitution, as president, he holds that office for a specified term only "and is made personally responsible [for his actions] by impeachment for his malfeasance in office." Taney didn't stop there. He scourged Lincoln further with the following words:

> *If the writ be usurped by the military power, at its discretion* [then] *the people of the United States are no longer living under a government of laws, but every citizen holds life, liberty and property at the will and pleasure of the army officer in whose military district he may be found.*

It was a lesson in constitutional law and American justice issued from the pen of the country's highest legal authority. But as Lincoln had done with the letters he had earlier received from Brown, Hicks and Garrett, he folded his arms across his chest, turned his back and ignored Taney's order to release Merryman. Merryman was later released, but not because of the court's order.

There was not much more Taney could do after severely lecturing the president. The United States Supreme Court lacked the power of enforcement, as Taney had already observed, As president and commander in chief, Abraham Lincoln controlled the armed forces of the United States of America, and he could pressure the secretary of justice to order his marshals to ignore future habeas corpus writs issued by judges of the country's Federal district courts.

The ends to which Lincoln might have been prepared to go to ensure the integrity of the Union were revealed by Brown in his memoir. He relates a conversation with Taney held on that day, after the hearing was concluded. Taney sat with Brown and told him that despite his position as chief justice of the Supreme Court, he, too, had been on the long list of persons to be arrested by the military but was advised that the authorities had relented and he was no longer in danger. Then he warned Brown that he was marked for arrest, which would soon occur. Taney's warning proved true. Brown would be arrested and spend time in Federal prisons, unable to attend to his duties as mayor of Baltimore. He was finally released in February 1862 at the end of his term.

Looking at the situation from the hindsight of a century and a half, it's clear that Lincoln had little choice. The Pratt Street Riot was no longer a local event concerning only Baltimore or even Maryland. It had developed into a serious national concern. The safety of the nation's capital lay within Lincoln's hands. As the nation's chief executive, he was charged with the responsibility of acting swiftly and decisively to prevent a national crisis and protect the country's citizens. The nation was in peril, its very being at stake. Lincoln was committed to preserving the Union and restoring the secessionists to their places in a unified America.

Although the rules surrounding habeas corpus and martial law were deeply set in the history and essence of Anglo-American law, Lincoln had no choice but to ignore them. It was a dangerous road to follow, yet as president he had few options. Habeas corpus was, as Winston Churchill once remarked, "a law which is above the king and which even he must not break." Lincoln, as America's "king," was breaking the law and expecting to succeed because he was invoking another and much older legal concept: the ancient Roman maxim used by the Caesars: *inter arma silent legis* (during war laws are silent).

The first communities to feel the bite of Lincoln's suspension of civil rights were, of course, Baltimore and parts of the state of Maryland, which fell to military control. Lincoln realized that he could not allow this geographically strategic state to be come part of the Confederacy. Lincoln was forced to arrest judges, newspaper editors and journalists sympathetic to the South, state legislators, police officials and any prominent civic leaders who openly demonstrated Southern bias or threatened to lead Maryland into the Confederacy.

The guidelines established for arrests were simple: one was liable to arrest if he gave or intended to give assistance to the enemy; if he discouraged enlistment in the Union army or encouraged someone to join the Confederacy; if he publicly showed Southern sympathy; if he criticized Lincoln or his administration; or if he belonged to a forbidden organization. Those unfortunates who were apprehended were denied access to legal counsel. It "was not waging war," Lincoln emphasized. "It was repressing a rebellion." When Lincoln struck his hammer-blow to Baltimore, it was to make certain that the Baltimore–Washington corridor would remain open and safe in order to permit his Union troops to move freely, without fear of attack, across the city. There could be no repeat of the Pratt Street Riot.

Some of the early arrests were dramatic. Frank Key Howard, the grandson of Baltimore icon Francis Scott Key and son of Baltimore's police commissioner, was arrested and imprisoned at Fort McHenry, the very place Key wrote about in his patriotic poem, "The Star Spangled Banner." Howard's crime was that he was the editor of Baltimore's pro-Southern *Baltimore Daily Exchange.*

The grandson of Major George Armistead, commander of Fort McHenry, who defended the fort against the British navy during the battle about which Key wrote, was also arrested and clapped into the fort's brig. His crime was that a Confederate flag was found in a traveling bag. By September, the military had arrested all the Maryland legislators known or suspected to be disloyal to the Union; Thomas Hall Jr., editor of the pro-Southern Baltimore newspaper *South*; and George Brown, the city's mayor.

Lincoln was ridding Maryland of its pro-Southern sympathizers. In Baltimore, aside from Mayor Brown and the two newspaper editors, military authorities had, on April 27, arrested, under authority of General Winfield Scott, Police Chief Kane. He was sent off to Fort McHenry and later shipped north to a fort in New York State. In letters he sent to Federal authorities, Kane complained of inhuman conditions leading to attacks of malaria. He

The Baltimore Light Artillery. *Courtesy of Enoch Pratt Free Library, Maryland's State Resource Center, Baltimore, MD.*

asked to be released. From all accounts, prison life was not pleasant; men were crowded together in their cells, and aside from his attacks of malaria, Kane noted his jailor's indifference to his personal toilet needs. Later he would complain of a heart condition. In all, thirty-one Maryland state legislators, together with congressmen, judges, public office holders, editors and private citizens were seized by the military and shuttled into prison without formal charges. For these men, the only way out was through a review by a military officer because Abraham Lincoln ensured that the writ of habeas corpus would be unavailable to this unhappy and powerless group who would be moved from Fort McHenry to a succession of prisons, such as Forts Lafayette and Warren in the North.

CHAPTER IX

The Story of Habeas Corpus

And by other shifts to avoid their yielding obedience to such writs [habeas corpus], *contrary to their duty and the known laws of the land, whereby many of the King's subjects have been and hereafter may be long detained in prison in such cases where by law bailable to their great charges and vexation.*
—Parliament's Habeas Corpus Act of 1679

In 1861, when Abraham Lincoln denied the citizens of Baltimore and Maryland the use of the writ of habeas corpus, it was the first time in the nation's history that any president had done so. Englishmen had already been enjoying that right for over six centuries. Less than a century earlier, Americans had enshrined the ancient English common law writ within the earliest documents of rights associated with the creation of their new nation. Article 1, Section 9 of the U.S. Constitution prohibited the suspension of habeas corpus except in cases of invasion, rebellion or if the maintenance of public safety so required it. The decision to suspend the guarantee, however, lies not with the president, as Justice Taney correctly pointed out, but with the nation's legislature: the Congress of the United States.

As subjects of the British Crown living in the thirteen colonies before the Revolutionary War, colonial Americans were also privileged to invoke the writ of habeas corpus with all of its long and distinguished history. It was one of the foundations of basic civil rights upon which all Englishmen could call no matter where they lived within the British Empire.

The writ's origins are part of England's early history. The idea of habeas corpus was born in 1215 on the boggy plains of a place known as

Runneymede, just outside of London. It was here that a band of English nobles met with their powerful monarch, King John. After pressuring and negotiating with John, they persuaded him to surrender some of his autocratic and unlimited powers. One of the concessions they wrung from him was to stop the practice of taking property and detaining noblemen without cause. The term "habeas corpus" does not appear in the first document, although the concept of arbitrary arrest was forbidden. It was the beginning of a centuries-slow erosion of the powers of the English monarchy.

The charter John was forced to sign was the famous Magna Carta or the "Great Charter." It became one of the foundations of Anglo-Saxon democracy. At first, the Magna Carta applied only to a small segment of English society: the barons, nobles and freedmen. The clause that prevented unwarranted arrests bloomed into a full judicial review for relief against the state's unlawful imprisonment or detention of a citizen. It was to become known in the legal community as the writ of habeas corpus.

The Magna Carta would be revised several times because, although he signed it, John never really intended to be bound by it. In 1297, after its final revision, the Magna Carta finally became the document that free people revere today. Unlawful imprisonment in the 1297 revision was covered in Clause 36. Eight years after its finalization, habeas corpus was invoked for the first time in an English court and would eventually apply to every Englishman, regardless of his or her station in society.

By 1679, the basis and use of the writ had seriously deteriorated and was being ignored and abused by the courts and jailers. Legislators noted this in the preamble to Parliament's Judiciary Act of 1679. They deplored the "great delays by gaolers, sheriffs and other officials." The Judiciary Act of 1679, titled "An Act for the Better Securing the Liberty of the Subject and for the Prevention of Imprisonment Beyond the Seas," did away with those inexcusable delays and forced custodians of persons claiming illegal imprisonment to surrender them, with all due speed, to a court for a hearing to determine the truth of their claims to freedom. Otherwise, as the act implied, during the delays, prisoners were sent to penal colonies abroad to be lost to the legal system forever. The Act of 1679 also gave the right of prisoners to request, and receive, bail pending trial.

A century later, Americans free of the English Crown but still heirs to English common law, passed their own version of England's Act of 1679. It was the Judiciary Act of 1789. One of its clauses also gave a prisoner the right to apply to a court for a writ of habeas corpus and have a judicial review to determine the legality of his imprisonment.

The act was needed because the U.S. Constitution only covered some aspects of the writ—invasion, rebellion and public safety—and was not explicit about a prisoner's rights under the writ in instances not covered by the Constitution. Nowhere is there a definition of an unlawful arrest, and Congress was limited to suspension of the writ in cases of rebellion, emergency and insurrection. Courts had to analyze each case on the facts surrounding the supposed illegal arrest. Today, habeas corpus applies not only to those instances set out in the Constitution and the Judiciary Act of 1797—those laws applied to government and public officials who were ordered to account for illegally detained prisoners—but its scope has also been extended to force private citizens to account for and produce persons they may be holding illegally, such as in child custody disputes.

Lincoln, as a young lawyer riding the circuits in the Illinois backcountry representing both civil and criminal clients, was surely aware of habeas corpus and its importance as a potent legal tool to guarantee a person's civil liberties. Now, after holding office for only a month, he was faced with the greatest crisis of any of his predecessors. Lincoln had to act quickly and decisively. That was why he invoked the Roman doctrine: "In war laws are silent."

Lincoln's orders were harsh for the citizens of Baltimore; they could be imprisoned at any time by an unfettered military. They lived under a battery of Union cannons perched atop Federal Hill. The cannons might open fire on them at any time for any reason, just or unjust in the eyes of the military, which had also installed armed camps in parks and other sensitive areas throughout the city. Baltimoreans hoped they would not be arbitrarily arrested for a chance remark or some misunderstood act as they carried on their daily lives along the city's streets or in their homes. They hoped they would not be roused from their beds in the early morning hours. They hoped they would not be detained for undetermined periods of time in dank cells jammed with other men and without any hope of judicial release. Lincoln, as he said, was not waging war but stopping a rebellion. It was toward this end that he issued Executive Order 100 on April 27, establishing martial law.

The geographic location indicated in Lincoln's order covered the area where Southern sympathizers had destroyed railroad tracks, bridges and telegraph wires, intending to cut Baltimore off from the North. What is curious, however, is another Lincoln order—Proclamation 82—issued around the same time. In this order, he mandated a naval blockade of the ports of South Carolina, Georgia, Florida, Alabama, Louisiana, Mississippi and Texas. Surely Lincoln, or at least one of his astute advisors or a cabinet member, must have known that under international law, ordering a naval blockade is deemed a declaration of war. To add to this ambiguous proclamation, Lincoln said that any man trying to run the blockade would be treated as a pirate. If a state of war existed between the Union and the CSA, a blockade runner would normally be treated as a privateer or a prisoner of war. A pirate faces the death penalty. In any case, at that stage of the war, the Union would have had a difficult time patrolling fifteen hundred miles of Atlantic coastline. Then there were the Gulf Coast ports of Florida, Mississippi, Louisiana and Texas. The Union lacked the naval power to do so. It was a strange order for a man who claimed to Mayor Brown and others that he was not as yet fighting a war.

By Order 1, "Relating to Political Prisoners," issued on February 14, 1862, the right of a citizen to request a court's review of his imprisonment by habeas corpus was reinstated. Reading Lincoln's reasons for its suspension a year earlier, one is struck by his apologetic tone with respect to how he chose to deal with the crisis the country was facing. But seven months later, on September 24, 1862, Lincoln suspended habeas corpus for a second time, again on his own and illegally. He offered as an explanation his concern that there might be resistance to his new Draft Act, an act of Congress designed to draft men into the army, as the military needed more men to replace its large losses on the battlefield. Congress passed the Draft Act on the same day as the Habeas Corpus Act (legitimizing Lincoln's illegal September suspension): March 3, 1863. Lincoln predicted a violent reaction to the Draft Act. If so, he would again have to act swiftly, as he had done earlier in Baltimore. This time, however, he would have complete authority from Congress.

As Lincoln correctly guessed, there was a bloody riot in New York City. The riots required a call for Union troops to control the situation. Compared to the New York Draft Riots, the Pratt Street Riot was a minor skirmish. Starting on Monday, July 13, 1863, the military had to battle with gangs of New Yorkers until Thursday, July 16, before they could finally contain the insurrection. Over 120 civilians died. Some say deaths were in the hundreds, and another 2,000 were wounded. To this day, it remains the largest insurrection in American history aside from the Civil War. Lincoln had learned from his Baltimore experience that suspending habeas corpus and imposing martial law was an unpopular but necessary means to control civilians.

With respect to his second suspension of habeas corpus, Lincoln took Justice Taney's good advice and had Congress legalize its suspension through legislative action. Sadly, the new act was not limited to Maryland or New York alone but was extended to cover all the states of the North.

Despite the severe sanctions placed on Baltimore, Federal authorities were still concerned about a fresh insurrection. Since under martial law the military did not need search warrants to enter, search and seize private property, soldiers began scouring the city for hidden weapons. They discovered that caches of arms had been stashed all around the city. These weapons could be an important factor should there be another uprising in Baltimore. Although the city's police had acted admirably during the riot by braving the mob to protect the soldiers of the Sixth Massachusetts, they were now under suspicion for their pro-Southern sympathies. That included their chief, George Kane, and members of the board of police commissioners as well.

A contingent of General Cadwalader's troops backed up a U.S. marshal who made a demand of Charles Howard, the president of the city's board of police commissioners, to give up a hidden cache of arms belonging to the city. They had been stored at the McKim House on Greenmount Avenue and in quantities much greater than the city would ever need. Under Police Chief Kane's reluctant supervision, wagons full of arms were carted away and delivered to Fort McHenry. A similar hoard of weapons was found in the basement of the Maryland Club, another well-known center of pro-Southern sympathy. Later, in a building in back of George Kane's police headquarters, a large supply of cannons, shot, pistols and muskets was found concealed in ceilings and walls. Also found was a large quantity of pikes, long poles upon which steel spears were mounted. These were manufactured by Ross Winans at Kane's request.

McHenry Howard, a member of the Maryland Militia, had hoarded some rifles he collected at the U.S. Armory but was afraid to bring them home, as this might implicate his older brother, Frank, and his father, Charles Howard, the police commissioner. The two were arrested anyway, and McHenry later found his way, shortly after the Pratt Street Riot, to service in the Confederate army. Captain Hare of the Sixth Massachusetts confronted Kane, formally demanding that the police chief return all the weapons and ammunition that had been abandoned by the fleeing soldiers during the riot. Undoubtedly, Kane had planned to add them to his very substantial arsenal.

On May 30, Governor Hicks, once again firmly in the Union camp, also arranged to have the state control its arms. He issued an order to Colonel E.R. Petherbridge directing him "to collect immediately all arms and

Captain Hare demands the return of his soldiers' arms collected by Marshal Kane after the riot. *Courtesy Enoch Pratt Free Library, Maryland's State Resource Center, Baltimore, MD.*

accoutrements belonging to the state of Maryland and hold the same in safekeeping subject to my orders."

If Baltimoreans were still plagued with nightmares at the harsh treatment they received under the stern hand of Benjamin F. Butler, there was to be no relief with the appointment of his successor, General Cadwalader, or, later, General John Adams Dix. The memory of the Pratt Street Riot was still fresh in the minds of the Union military, and Dix was determined to prevent any new riots in the territory of his newly assigned command.

After taking over the Baltimore Military District, Dix made an assessment of the fortifications at Fort McHenry and Federal Hill. He realized they were vulnerable to a land attack and promptly beefed them up, adding several other campsites around the city. He needed new fortifications for the large number of troops he brought into the city. As was Lincoln, Dix was aware of Baltimore's importance to the defense of Washington. He added more troops to the five thousand he commanded upon assuming military control of the city. No longer were Baltimoreans permitted to display the Confederate colors or Confederate song sheets that were freely being displayed and sold in Northern cities. Federal Hill was transformed from Butler's quickly thrown-together encampment into an impressive fort.

Despite his eagerness to make many arrests, probably to keep Baltimoreans on their best behavior, Dix still insisted that his officers state a good case for the arrest of wrongdoers. And Dix would not authorize the search of a civilian's private home. On more than one occasion, he released prisoners because the reasons for their arrest were either shaky or nonexistent. And he seems to have had a sense of justice because he was aware that some persons remained in prisons, "overlooked" or forgotten for long periods, without good reason. Nevertheless, it was under his administration that the wholesale arrests of Maryland legislators, including Baltimore's mayor, George Brown, and former governor Thomas Pratt were executed. Some historians assert that either Lincoln or Secretary of State William Seward ordered Dix to make the arrests. Dix, like Butler before him, fell out of favor and was dismissed from his post under fire for the brutal treatment dealt to Easton's Judge Richard Carmichael when he was arrested.

But Baltimore would still enjoy no relief from the military's heavy-handed treatment. Dix's successor, John E. Wool, showed even less compassion; he resumed the abandoned practice of invading private homes, searching them and seizing such property as he deemed contraband, and stepped up arrests, including those of women. The War Department and cabinet members were constantly pressuring the military to arrest, try and punish any disloyal acts, utterances or interference with the recruitment of soldiers. They were to be quickly and summarily dealt with.

CHAPTER X

Baltimore

A Prisoner of Its Geography

Remember the cells of Fort McHenry! Remember
The dungeons of Fort Lafayette and Fort Warren!
The insults to your wives and daughters—the arrests
The midnight searches of your houses!
Remember these your wrongs, and rise at once in arms
And strike for Liberty and Right!
—*Part of a recruitment poster issued in 1862 by Colonel Bradley T. Johnson, CSA*

D uring the Civil War, the Confederate army was also aware of Baltimore's unique geographic location with respect to Washington. The CSA knew that the city continued to harbor a large group of Southern sympathizers, some of whom continued to slip across the Potomac to join the Confederate army. Maryland supplied regiments that fought in both the Union and Confederate armies. There are monuments at Gettysburg to remind Americans of that fact. And even today, Maryland's 175th Infantry flies the Confederate flag as one of its regimental standards.

Although many of the city's important and influential leaders had been arrested by the military, many of the five thousand Baltimoreans who had marched out to Pratt Street on that April day were still free and at large in the city. During the war, at least two attempts were made to break Baltimore and Maryland away from the Union. Each was, of course, unsuccessful.

In May 1862, as a Confederate army was preparing itself for battle against the Union army in Manassas, Virginia, and the city was in no danger, the First Maryland Volunteers, infantrymen attached to Stonewall Jackson's

Union troops occupying the main post office at Gay and Lombard Streets. *Courtesy Enoch Pratt Free Library, Maryland's State Resource Center, Baltimore, MD.*

Headquarters of the Third Maryland Veteran Volunteers. *Courtesy Enoch Pratt Free Library, Maryland's State Resource Center, Baltimore, MD.*

army, were looking to the north and nearby Baltimore. The city was always on their mind. Maryland's soldiers sitting around their campfires sang:

Baltimore ain't you happy,
We'll anchor by and by,
We'll stand the storm, it won't be long,
We'll anchor by and by.

It took two more invasions into Northern territory by a substantial Confederate force to remind Baltimore's citizenry and Lincoln that the South still considered the city an important prize. After the Pratt Street Riot, the city still faced danger by Confederate attempts to cut the strategic line between it and Washington.

The first try was in July 1863 at the Battle of Gettysburg, when Confederate general Robert E. Lee pushed through Maryland into Pennsylvania and was scarcely sixty miles from Baltimore. The second and much more serious venture occurred a year later, almost to the day, when Lee sent General Jubal Early to invade Washington. Part of this grand strategy was to repeat the plan of cutting the lines between Washington and Baltimore. Lee sought to relieve pressure on a beleaguered Richmond under siege by the Union army. He wanted to force a political solution to the war and divert Union troops from Richmond. To accomplish this, Lee devised a bold strategy.

General Early was charged with dismantling the same rails, telegraphs and highways destroyed on the night of the Pratt Street Riot. Early split his forces in two. One force, led by Early, was to head for Washington. The other, led by Frederick's General Bradley T. Johnson and Baltimore's Major Harry Gilmor, was ordered to harass and destroy the Baltimore infrastructure. Gilmor was to remain in the Baltimore area and continue interfering with and destroying railroad operations and telegraph communications. Johnson was ordered to help Gilmor in Baltimore and then push on to the prison camp at Point Lookout, Maryland. The prison camp was located at the farthest southwest corner of the western side of the state, where the Potomac empties into the Chesapeake Bay. Point Lookout held about fifteen thousand Confederate prisoners captured a year earlier at Gettysburg. Lee hoped to free them so that they could be armed and then marched on to Washington to strengthen Early's army. Once Baltimore was shut down, invading Washington would be easy, as no help could come from the North.

Early actually penetrated the outskirts of Washington. His riflemen could see and actually fire at President Lincoln, who stood atop one of the city's forts watching the skirmish. Early was forced to retreat when Grant sent reinforcements by steamer from Virginia to repel the invaders. Early might have succeeded in reaching Washington had he kept to his timetable. He arrived a day late, his army held up by Union forces led by General Lew Wallace.

From his post in Baltimore, Wallace, who was commander of the Eighth Army Corps stationed in the city, sensed the danger and, as Butler had, acted quickly and sometimes without authority. He originally commanded a force of only thirty-five hundred soldiers. He had to slap together a patchwork army of over five thousand to oppose Early. Then he rushed his troops by John Garrett's B&O trains to Monocacy, just outside Baltimore, where, outnumbered three to one, he boldly placed them in front of Jubal Early's advancing army. Wallace lost the battle, but he delayed Early, Johnson and Gilmor by one precious day. At first, Wallace's efforts were dismissed by General Grant. In a few weeks, after his action was properly assessed, Wallace became a hero, credited with saving both Washington and Baltimore by delaying Early that one important day. Grant would finally acknowledge that had Early been at Washington a day sooner, the city would have been in grave peril.

Baltimore's citizens barricading the streets against a possible Confederate invasion from Gettysburg, 1863. *Courtesy of Enoch Pratt Free Library, Maryland's State Resource Center, Baltimore, MD.*

Early, Gilmor and Johnson made their retreat south across the Potomac into Virginia. Johnson was assigned to cover Early's rear flank. His troops were assaulted by the cannons of the Baltimore Light Artillery, which lobbed shells at escaping Confederate wagons.

Lee might have been counting on a sympathetic population in Baltimore to ease Early's invasion, but that did not happen. Although there were still many Southern sympathizers in the city, Lincoln and his military occupation had gone a long way to pacify Baltimore since the outset of the Pratt Street Riot. Proof was shown a year earlier, when Lee invaded Maryland on his way to Gettysburg in Pennsylvania. In addition to sending all of New York's militia to Baltimore on June 23, 1863, General Sanford was ordered by the secretary of war to order New York's Sixth and Fifty-fifth Regiments to protect the city. The newly arrived soldiers were met with concerned citizens piling up barricades around strategic parts of the city. The barricades were not for the Yankee soldiers of New York. They were meant to shut out Robert E. Lee's Confederate army.

Chapter XI

Lincoln's Last Ride

*The Aftermath of the Pratt Street Riot,
April 21, 1865, to Present*

*Most Marylanders find it difficult to answer the question. Some consider themselves
Southerners; others as Northerners. Perhaps the truth lies between the extremes.
—Answer by the Maryland Department of State in 1956 to the query, "Is the state
Southern or Northern?"*

Aside from the important role it played during the Pratt Street Riot, the
B&O's Camden Station in southwest Baltimore has historic roots in the
Civil War and with President Abraham Lincoln in particular. It was the final
leg for the Sixth Massachusetts soldiers on their way to Washington. It was
at the telegraph office of the B&O that news of the attack on Fort Sumter
was first received a week earlier.

Lincoln passed through Camden Yards, as president, on at least three
historic occasions. The first was on February 23, 1861, on his way to
Washington for his presidential inauguration. He changed trains at Calvert
Station to get to Camden.

His second passage occurred in 1863, when he traveled on his way to
Pennsylvania to deliver the historic Gettysburg address. The rail lines, which
had been destroyed by Confederate soldiers, had to be hastily repaired to
allow the president to proceed on.

Finally, after Lincoln's assassination on April 21, 1865, the funeral cortege,
which traveled from Washington to Springfield, Illinois, made its first stop at
Camden Yards. The cortege was made up of nine railroad cars of the B&O,
on which the company's president, John Garrett, was a passenger. Lincoln
made his last trip resting in his private car, which was painted a chocolate

brown on the outside and bore a federal coat of arms with outstretched eagle's wings. The coach was draped in black mourning cloth. As the train worked its way north, bonfires were lit along the tracks, and church bells tolled sadly. Railroad workers guarded road crossings, and the steady boom of saluting cannons could be heard throughout the countryside.

At 10:00 a.m., Lincoln's body was removed from Camden Yards to the Merchants Exchange at Gay and Water Streets, only a few short paces from Pratt Street, where one of his earliest crises as president arose. At the Merchants Exchange, Lincoln's casket was opened, and he lay in state for mourners to view. The casket was then removed to the Howard Street Station at 2:00 p.m., when it continued its sad journey to Illinois using the Northern Central Railroad. The citizens of Baltimore had come to terms with their late president, the majority of them having voted for his reelection.

The effects of the Pratt Street Riot did not end with Lincoln's death or the South's surrender. There is a book entitled *Maryland: The South's First Casualty*. There is much truth to that statement. Maryland remained a casualty for a long time after the end of the Civil War. It was the first to feel the effects of martial law and the suspension of habeas corpus. Throughout the entire war, Maryland, and especially Baltimore, lived beneath the cannon and the rifle, its citizens subject to capricious arrest and imprisonment. After the war, Baltimore continued to suffer along with the rest of the South. While it did not undergo the physical devastation of Atlanta or other Southern cities, it fell into an economic decline. Its main markets, located in the South, had shriveled as Southern states struggled to return to normal, lacking the cash to buy Baltimore's products.

In an article in the *Baltimore Sun* by Frederick N. Rasmussen, an astute observer of Baltimore and Maryland history, he cites historian Gerald W. Johnson, who detailed the demise of Baltimore for four decades after the Civil War. It was, in Johnson's words, a "Biblical Abomination of Desolation by the utter destruction" of the city's trading partners. Baltimore continued showing its Southern face by maintaining segregation until the civil rights movement ended that practice in the 1960s.

By the end of the nineteenth century, Baltimore had strengthened its manufacturing muscle once again, making steel in its furnaces and setting keels for ships to be used in the American Merchant Navy. Throughout, it maintained its southern profile. Although Maryland's sons had fought on both sides during the war, Confederate war memorials were set throughout the city. Not until 1909 did the city erect one celebrating those Marylanders who fought for the Union.

"Maryland, My Maryland" still contains bitter anti-Lincoln and anti-Union stanzas that thousands upon thousands of the state's schoolchildren have learned and sung since 1939. That was the year it was adopted as Maryland's state anthem. Repeated efforts by the state legislature to eliminate those words have been unsuccessful, and every once in a while someone makes a joking reference to "Mob Town."

Some vestiges of the Pratt Street Riot's legacy remain with us, even after a century and a half.

APPENDIX I

The Lives of Some of the
Participants After the Pratt Street
Riot and the Civil War

A fter the Civil War, Maryland slowly returned to normal. The city, after
some decades, eventually resumed and even exceeded its prewar role as
an important industrial, railroading and maritime center. The later careers
of the major actors who tried unsuccessfully to steer the state on a course of
secession, and those who successfully prevented it, demonstrate the nation's
ability to heal the wounds and scars of one of America's bloodiest wars, as
every man killed or wounded on the battlefield was an American. Maryland
succeeded in warmly embracing those who tried to wrest her from the Union.

MAYOR GEORGE BROWN: After spending the rest of his mayoral term in
prison, Brown was released at Boston in December 1862. He returned to
Baltimore, where, after the war, he was elected chief justice of the Supreme
Bench of Baltimore. He served on the board of many important Baltimore
institutions, such as the Peabody Institute, the Johns Hopkins University and
the Maryland Historical Society. In 1887, conscious that he was growing
older and wishing to retain a record of the event, Brown wrote his personal
account of the Pratt Street Riot: *Baltimore the Nineteenth of April 1861*. Brown
died in 1890.

GENERAL BENJAMIN F. BUTLER: Switching from the Democratic to the
Republican Party, Butler was elected to the House of Representatives from
1867 to 1876 with a short break in the middle. He managed the unsuccessful
impeachment proceedings against President Andrew Johnson. He went on
to coauthor America's first comprehensive civil rights legislation, which was

later declared unconstitutional. Butler became governor of Massachusetts in 1883. Despite his difficult personality, his administration was noted for appointing minorities, including African Americans and women, to high office. He tried unsuccessfully to get the presidential nomination in 1884.

GENERAL JOHN A. DIX: Dix served as America's minister to France from 1866 to 1869. He was New York's governor from 1873 to 1876. The New Jersey military post, Fort Dix, is named for him.

CIPRIANO FERRANDINI: Although thought to be a conspirator in the 1861 plot to assassinate Lincoln and an outspoken Southern sympathizer, Ferrandini was not arrested that year. He was finally detained in 1862 and then released almost immediately. He continued operating his barbershop at Barnum's Hotel until 1870. He lived a quiet and uneventful life, always denying any role in a Lincoln assassination plot. Ferrandini died in 1910.

MAJOR HARRY GILMOR: Gilmor repeated his role in the destruction of Baltimore's railroads and telegraphs in a failed attempt by Confederate forces to cut off Baltimore and Washington from the Union in July 1864. After the war, Gilmor settled in his Baltimore home at Glen Ellen, near Loch Raven. He rose to become a colonel in the Maryland National Guard and then police commissioner of Baltimore from 1874 to 1879. In 1866, he wrote *Four Years in the Saddle*, an autobiographical account of his wartime service in the Confederate cavalry.

GOVERNOR THOMAS HICKS: Appointed U.S. senator for Maryland in 1862 to fill a vacancy, Hicks successfully ran for reelection in 1864 but died in 1865. Abraham Lincoln attended the funeral held in the Capitol Building, two months before his own assassination.

GENERAL BRADLEY JOHNSON: In July 1864, Maryland native Johnson commanded the cavalry unit assigned by General Jubal Early to destroy Baltimore's infrastructure in an unsuccessful attempt at cutting off Washington from the North. Johnson was Harry Gilmor's superior. Johnson never returned to Maryland. Unlike most of his colleagues, he lived the rest of his days in Virginia, where he practiced law.

POLICE COMMISSIONER GEORGE P. KANE: Released from a Federal prison in 1862, he went to Montreal, where he plotted unsuccessfully to release

Confederate prisoners in an Ohio prison camp. Kane advanced several wild schemes to liberate Baltimore from the Union, none of which was ever seriously considered. Kane returned to Baltimore in 1870 and served on the Jones Falls Commission. He was elected Baltimore's sheriff from 1871 to 1873 and then mayor in 1877. He died while in office in 1878.

ABRAHAM LINCOLN: Lincoln was reelected to office in 1864 by a much wider margin than his 1860 election. He even posted a majority in Maryland. After learning of Robert E. Lee's surrender at Appomattox, Lincoln had little time to enjoy his victories. He was assassinated by John Wilkes Booth at Washington's Ford's Theatre on April 14, 1865, little more than a month after his second inauguration and five days after Appomattox.

ISAAC RIDGEWAY TRIMBLE: At age sixty-one, the fiery secessionist became the oldest and one of the boldest generals in the Confederate army. He was said to have been a favorite of the legendary Stonewall Jackson. Trimble lost a part of his left leg at Gettysburg in an action associated with Pickett's Charge. He was then captured and remained a prisoner until 1865. He was denied parole despite his wounds because the Union was aware of his expert knowledge of railroads. At the war's end, he returned to Baltimore to continue with his railroading career.

GENERAL LEW WALLACE: The man who patched together his tiny Baltimore command to delay the invasion of Baltimore and Washington in 1864 was a politician and lawyer. After the war, he served on the court-martial board that tried some of Lincoln's assassins. He was appointed governor of the New Mexico Territory during the same time Billy the Kid engaged in the range wars. He was later appointed minister to the Ottoman Empire. While governor of New Mexico, Wallace wrote the bestseller *Ben Hur*, which was made into a movie several times.

ROSS WINANS: After the war, the wealthy Winans traveled between England and Russia with his son and continued to devote himself to building vessels and arranging to construct railroads. He died in England in 1877.

Pratt Street Riot Markers

S ix markers commemorating the Pratt Street Riot have been installed by
the Maryland Historical Trust, starting at the President Street Station
and proceeding on to Pratt Street and then on to Camden Station. They
cover the distance of the more than a mile and a half that the men of the
Sixth Massachusetts had to march in order to reach Camden Station. The
markers explain many of the dramatic events occurring at the exact locations
along the route taken by soldiers of the Sixth Massachusetts.

MARKER ONE: The march started here at the President Street Station at
PRESIDENT and FLEET STREETS, located in the neighborhood now known
as Harbor East. Once America's largest rail station, the building boasted a
long, enclosed transit shed that ran a considerable distance from the rear of
the two-story terminal that still remains. Originally built by Isaac Trimble
for the PW&B line, it was one of the connecting links between Baltimore
and Philadelphia. What remains is the oldest big-city terminal still extant,
and it is listed on the National Register of Historic Places. Today, the last
structure is the location of the Civil War Museum

In 1861, the neighborhood was given over to railroading and other
industry. Today, it is a different neighborhood transformed by Baltimore's
urban renewal. Nearby streets are lined with upscale condominiums,
shops, hotels and some of the city's finest restaurants. The old depot
building has been used as the Civil War Museum. It has been in danger
both physically and by those who wish to convert the valuable property
into commercial space.

A street marker covering the route of the Pratt Street Riot. *Photograph courtesy of Marcus Dagan.*

Late in the morning on the nineteenth, Colonel Edward F. Jones, leading his Sixth Massachusetts, arrived at this station. He had already received a warning that there would be trouble upon his arrival. Nine cars were prepared to move the soldiers on Camden Station, along railway tracks that curved from President to Pratt Street around to the west side of the harbor, then known as "the Basin," and then south to Camden Yards. Jones led the cars from this location, proceeding on to Pratt Street, at first without incident. Captain A.S. Follansbee, who was in command of four companies, followed in the last car.

MARKER TWO: As Follansbee and his men left in their cars, they encountered a mob on PRATT STREET that had covered the railway tracks with sand, an anchor and tools blocking the last car's passage. Unable to proceed safely by car, Follansbee ordered his men back to President Street. Once back on President Street, he received orders from Colonel Jones to proceed on foot to Camden Yards. MARKER TWO, located at PRESIDENT and FAWN STREETS, just a few blocks north of the station, relates (out of chronological order) to the attacks on Follansbee's men as they were proceeding, for the second time, now on foot, to Camden Station. It was here that the first violent assaults were made against this group. On this spot, Lieutenant Leander Lynde courageously stepped into the crowd and tore the flag of South Carolina away from a demonstrator. Today, the neighborhood known as Little Italy is located on the east side of Fawn Street.

MARKER THREE: making a left turn on to PRATT STREET, at PRESIDENT and PRATT STREETS, the third marker is one block in near the JONES FALLS BRIDGE. It was here that Major Benjamin Watson became stalled when his car, the eighth in line, was loaded with four companies of men. The men were derailed by many objects, including a cannon that had been dragged along the tracks by demonstrators. Watson continued on when he forced the train's frightened operator, at gunpoint, to restore the car to the rails. It was at this point that Colonel Jones, learning that Captain Follansbee had to return to President Street, ordered him to proceed on foot following the railway route to Camden Station.

MARKER FOUR: PRATT STREET between GAY and COMMERCE STREETS. At this spot, an anchor was dragged by some sympathetic sailors from the nearby GAY STREET DOCK and placed across the rails. A rioter got hold of a rifle and fired into the column of the Massachusetts Sixth. A demonstrator was badly wounded as he tried taking away the regimental flag from one of the marching soldiers. Today, the Pratt Street Pavilion, part of the Inner Harbor complex, lines the waterfront where warehouses and dock sheds once stood.

MARKER FIVE: PRATT AND LIGHT STREETS. At this location, the harbor ended at its western corner. The violence toward Follansbee and his men on foot escalated greatly. Two soldiers were shot dead, while another was beaten to death by the mob. A fourth soldier would die after he was struck in the head by a stone. Accompanying the soldiers was a Baltimore police officer who had bravely joined them at Fawn Street. He advised Follansbee that they were close to Camden Station. Mayor Brown was, at this time, also alongside the Sixth Massachusetts trying to calm the mob. This scene of death and

The President Street Station as it appears today. *Photograph courtesy of Marcus Dagan.*

anger, 150 years ago, is contrasted today by the lovely Myerhoff Fountain peacefully flowing at the nearby Light Street Pavilion.

MARKER SIX: CAMDEN STATION. Here, at the last leg of their ordeal, the soldiers were besieged by a mob growing more menacing. As the rioters waved Southern banners and cheered for the South, Follansbee's companies hastened to link up with their comrades who had preceded them and waited for them to board the trains destined for Washington. Today, the station is a sports museum, and nearby Camden Yards is the home field of the Baltimore Orioles. To see the last marker, walk into the museum through the Pratt Street entrance. Here you will see two massive wooden benches, relics from their days of service in the terminal's waiting room. Go straight through the museum to the exit on the other side and then turn left. The last marker has been placed at a small dip by a grassy plot. An iron fence separates a path from the street. Here, Baltimore's modern Light Rail train runs along the same route where once the B&O's rail lines traveled south to Washington. The soldiers, after loading aboard their trains, left from this spot at 1:30 p.m. after a harrowing few hours. They were now on their way to help defend the nation's capital.

Sources and Materials Used in Research

BOOKS

Abdill, George B. *Civil War Railroads*. New York: Bonanza Books, 1961.

Brands, H.W. *Andrew Jackson*. New York: Anchor Books, 2005.

Brown, George William. *Baltimore & The Nineteenth of April, 1861*. Baltimore, MD: Johns Hopkins University, 1887. Reprint, 2001.

Clark, Charles Branch. *Politics in Maryland During the Civil War*. Chestertown, MD, 1952.

Cottom, Robert I., Jr., and Mary Ellen Hayward. *Maryland in the Civil War: A House Divided*. Baltimore: Maryland Historical Society, 1994.

Denton, Lawrence M. *A Southern Star for Maryland: Maryland and the Secession Crisis, 1860–1861*. Baltimore, MD: Publishing Concepts, Baltimore, 1995.

Donald, David Herbert. *Lincoln*. New York: Random House, 1998.

Farrell, Michael R. *Who Made All Our Street Cars Go?* Baltimore, MD: Baltimore NRHS Publications, 1973.

Fee, Elizabeth, Linda Shopes and Linda Zeidman. *The Baltimore Book: New Views of Local History*. Philadelphia: Temple University Press, 1991.

Fein, Isaac M. *The Making of an American Jewish Community: The History of Baltimore Jewry from 1773 to 1920*. Baltimore: Jewish Historical Society of Maryland, 1985.

Gilmor, Harry, Colonel. *Four Years in the Saddle*. New York: Harper Bros., 1866.

Howard, McHenry. *Reflections of a Maryland Confederate Soldier and Staff Officer under Johnston, Jackson and Lee*. Baltimore, MD: Williams and Wilkins Co., 1914.

Huntsberry, Thomas V., and Joanne M. Huntsberry. *The Second Maryland Battalion in the Civil War: Book I The South*. Baltimore, MD: J. Mart Publishing, 1985.

Korn, Bertram W. *American Jewry and the Civil War*. Philadelphia: Jewish Publication Society, 1951.

Markle, Donald E. *Spies and Spymasters of the Civil War*. New York: Hippocrene Books, 1994.

Mitchell, Alexander D., IV. *Baltimore Then and Now*. San Diego, CA: Thunder Bay Press, 2002.

Radcliffe, George L. *Governor Thomas Hicks of Maryland and the Civil War*. Baltimore, MD: Johns Hopkins Press, November–December 1901.

Talbert, Bart Rhett. *Maryland: The South's First Casualty*. Rockbridge, VA: Rockbridge Publishing Co., 1995.

Toomey, Daniel Carroll. *The Civil War in Maryland*. Baltimore, MD: Toomey Press, 1983.

Woodward, C. Vann. *Mary Chesnut's Civil War*. New Haven, CT: Yale University Press, 1981.

OTHER SOURCES

Anderson, Robert, Major. Reports submitted regarding the action at Fort Sumter to Simon Cameron, secretary of war, April 18, 1861, and to Colonel L. Thomas, adjutant general, April 19, 1861. Civil War Archive, 1861 Battle Reports.

Baltimore Sun, 1861, 1863, 1864. [The *Sun* carried reports of the Pratt Street Riot in 1861 and the reactions to a possible invasion in 1863, when General R.E. Lee invaded Pennsylvania at Gettysburg, and again in 1864, when General Jubal Early's army attacked both Baltimore and Washington.]

Brave, Ralph. "Baltimore, The Civil War and the Lasting Legacy of the Pratt Street Riots." *City Paper*, April 18, 2001.

British Parliament. Judiciary Act of 1697. "An Act for Better Securing the Liberty of the Subject for Prevention of Imprisonment Beyond the Seas." [The act of the British Parliament reforming and strengthening habeas corpus and extending bail to prisoners.]

Examiner.com. "The Gangs of Baltimore." May 22, 2007.

Ford, Martin. "The Gangs of Baltimore." *Humanities* 29, no. 3 (May/June 2008).

Jones, Colonel Edward F. *Conflict in Baltimore, MD.* Report prepared by Colonel Edward F. Jones and forwarded to Brigade Major William H. Clemence at Washington, D.C., April, 22, 1861.

Magna Carta. [The document that first dealt with habeas corpus in English common law. There are several amended versions after the original of 1215. The version usually referred to is the final one, prepared in 1297.]

Maryland Historical Society. "Maryland Online Encyclopedia." mdoe.org.

New York Times. "Enlistment Is for the War." April 18, 1861. [An account of the march in New York City of the Sixth Massachusetts.]

Rasmussen, Frederick N. "Are We Northern? Southern? Yes." *Baltimore Sun,* March 3, 2010.

Taney, Roger Brooke. Chief Justice's landmark decision in *ex parte Merryman.* 17 Fed. Cases 144 (C.C. MD., 1861).

U.S. Congress. Judiciary Act of 1797. [The Act of the United States Congress with clauses respecting habeas corpus.]

Wooley, John, and Gerhard Peters. *The Documents and Papers of Abraham Lincoln.* U.S. Department of State. [The complete collection of orders and proclamations issued by President Lincoln during his term in office is available here.]

About the Author

Harry A. Ezratty was born in New York City. He is a graduate of New York University and Brooklyn Law School. A maritime lawyer by profession, Harry is an independent history scholar. He has authored four books. His first, *How to Collect and Protect Works of Art*, was followed by three books covering historical subjects: *500 Years in the Jewish Caribbean*, *They Led the Way* and *The Builders*. Harry lectures extensively and teaches American Jewish history at Howard Community College in Maryland. After living and practicing law in Puerto Rico for thirty-five years, he returned to the mainland, settling in Baltimore, where he became interested in the city's rich history, especially the Pratt Street Riot. Harry is married to Barbara Tasch, a journalist, editor and publisher who grew up in Baltimore.

Visit us at
www.historypress.net